JADED

Rediscovering Hope in Reality

MIKE HARDER

Published by LifeWay Press®
© 2007 Mike Harder

ISBN: 978-1415-8627-11
Item: 005107925

Dewey Decimal Classification Number: 248.83
Subject Heading: CHRISTIAN LIFE \ IDEALISM \ CYNICISM

Printed in the United States of America.

Leadership and Adult Publishing
LifeWay Church Resources
One LifeWay Plaza
Nashville, Tennessee 37234-0175

We believe the Bible has God for its author; salvation for its end; and truth, without any mixture of error, for its matter and that all Scripture is totally true and trustworthy. The 2000 statement of The Baptist Faith and Message is our doctrinal guideline.

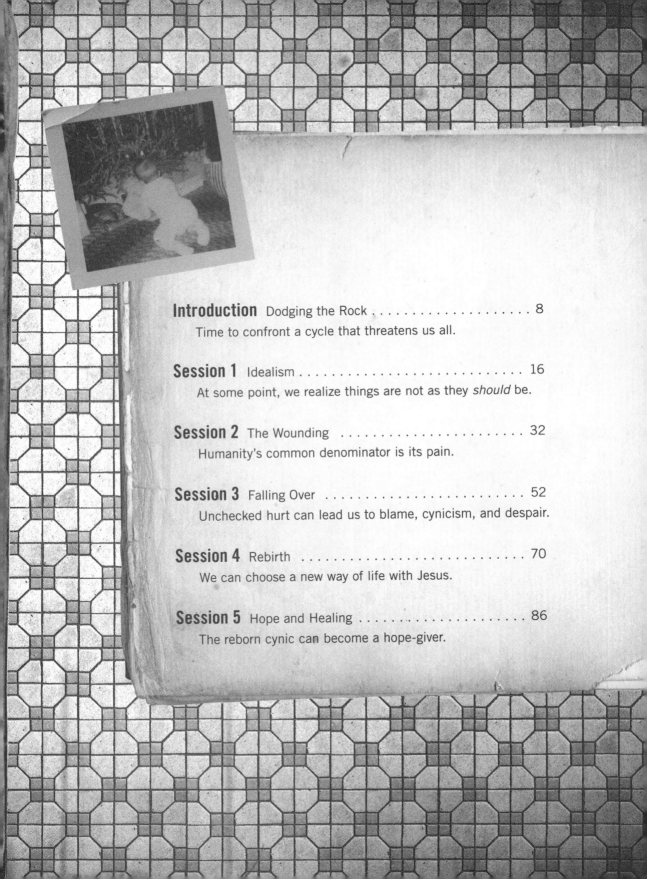

MEET THE AUTHOR

My name is Mike Harder, and I'm pretty much a normal guy who enjoys coffee (lots of coffee), wakeboarding, and several other sports. To know anything about me, you have to know the context of my life: I'm a missionary kid from Bogota, Colombia, where my parents served for twenty-eight years as church planters. I love being from Colombia, but God has called me to serve in the United States—it's my mission field. I am currently part of a new church in Nashville, Tennessee. Green Hills Church is a community that values accepting people as they are and walking with them toward maturity in Christ.

Before moving to Nashville, I earned a Master of Divinity from Mid-America Baptist Theological Seminary in Memphis, Tennessee. In addition to serving as co-pastor at Green Hills Church, I have opportunities to speak nationally through Mike Harder Ministries. In all of this, I'm motivated to make an impact on the spiritual condition and health of my generation, and I believe God can use Jaded to help make it happen. Come by and visit me at mikeharderministries.com or check out greenhillschurch.org.

Mike Harder

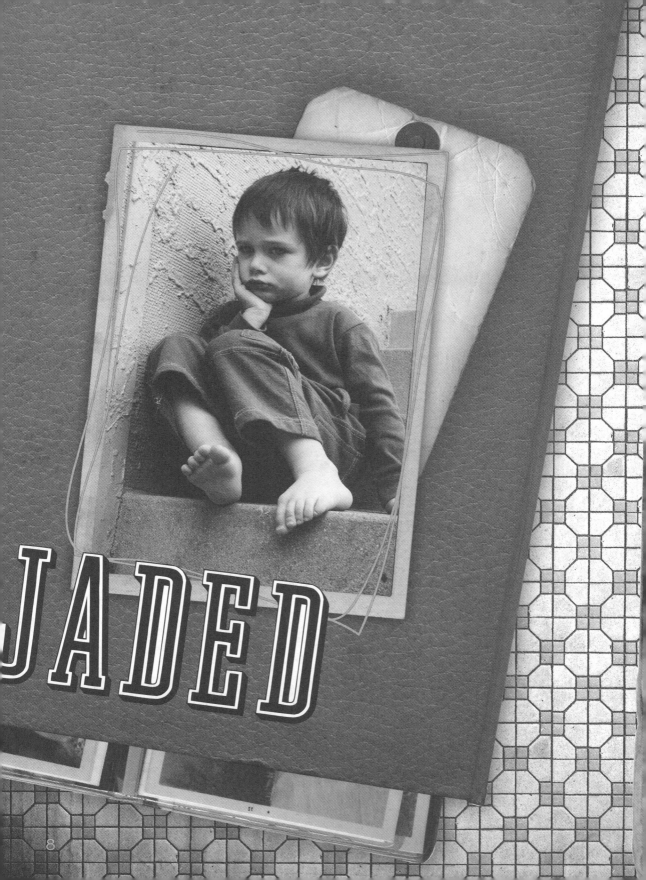

JADED

Dodging the Rock

I love white-water rafting.

Last summer my dad and I went on a father-son adventure in northern Wisconsin. The first day on our week-long trip, we hit the river in a boat with two other friends looking for adventure. As we were pushing off, our river guide, Sam, told us, "Guys, you really only need to watch out for one rock."

That particular boulder—a monster the size of a small car—was appropriately named Volkswagen Rock.

We headed down river and entered the gorge, synchronizing our paddle strokes and paddling hard to the right. At first it looked like we were going to pass through easily. Then, his voice cracking with fear, Sam screamed, "Hard left! Hard left!" The current was dragging us straight toward Volkswagen Rock. Everything blurred together for a few seconds. Sam shouted. Then Sam gurgled. Water passed over us. Five grown men began screaming and our raft collided with stone. Then there was only the deafening sound of rushing water.

When I opened my eyes, I was alone in what had once been the raft. Our boat had become blue graffiti on a rock wall, the same rock wall I was pinned to by the current. I took inventory to make sure my arms and legs were still attached; then I started laughing hysterically. Other rafters were pointing at us, and my father and our friends were freaking out while being swept down river in complete defeat. I had no choice but to launch myself into the rapids and join them.

After my adrenaline normalized, a thought came to mind: As much as we try to make life work for us, eventually we get shipwrecked on the rocks. Further, those rocks that capsize our lives often come out of nowhere. Things are going along smoothly at work, in our relationships, at church, and then we suddenly find ourselves struggling to catch our breath.

The question is not *if* something like that will happen to you—it will. You will become hurt in relationships. Your job will not be perfect. Your church will let you down. The real question is, "How will you respond when you discover the huge difference between your idealistic expectations and reality?

FEELING JADED?

Time and time again, things in life don't turn out like we planned. And when life fails to meet our expectations, we all run the risk of falling into an uncomfortable state of being we didn't plan for. We may look up one day to find that we're jaded.

Webster's defines *jaded* in two ways:

- **As an adjective, *jaded* means "fatigued by overwork; exhausted."**
- **As a verb, it means "to tire or dull through repetition or excess."**

Those words ring true, at least in my own life. Being jaded feels something like this: You used to be sharp—excited about life's possibilities, ready to cut a new trail in your relationships or or ministry or career. But along the way, life took away that sharpness and left you dull. In terms of this study, then, I think we can define *jaded* as "having the condition of cynicism and bitterness with pain at the root."

Have you given up hope that life will get any better? If so, you might be jaded.

All of us have gone through experiences that lead to becoming cynical and bitter. We haven't found the right love. We haven't landed the job. Our parents have failed us. Someone has broken our heart. Our dreams haven't come true. Add yours to the list. Many of us have been disappointed by our circumstances, but we don't have to remain there. There is life—*good* life—even after our ideals collide with reality. I think together we can find the way out of disillusionment, through reality, and back to hope.

IS GOD EVER DISAPPOINTED?

Hitting a jaded state can feel pretty lonely. There's one thing for sure, though: You are not the first to experience disappointment. The Bible deals with all kinds of people who faced disillusionment and frustration, and it offers countless stories of heartache and disaster. Surprisingly enough, the One who has encountered these things most in Scripture is God Himself. Throughout the Bible, He has dealt with failures of the people He loves. Although it is easy to think that God is untouchable, unreachable, and removed from everything here on earth, the Bible paints a very different picture.

The God we see in the Bible is an emotionally interactive being who genuinely feels emotions similar to our own. He has become injured emotionally through the actions and behavior of His children. This idea is not an example of us projecting our emotions onto God; instead, it's understanding that our emotions are a reflection of who God is. After all, we were created in His image. Even God can become discouraged. Why? It's because He has given us choices, and He has high hopes for what we will do with those choices. He wants us to achieve His blueprint for abundant life. The problem comes when we put aside His plan and pick up our own plans for what we think will make us happy.

THE PURSUIT OF HAPPINESS

Everyone wants to be happy. I know I do. In fact, most of the major life decisions I make are because I think the solution I choose will bring me greater happiness than my current situation does. I may try to get a job that pays more because I think the prestige and success and money will make me happier. I may try to date because I think having that person will make me happy. I have left a job and a city and a relationship—all because I thought it would make me happier. I have consistently found myself tying circumstances to happiness.

One time I thought that a dream car would make me happier (or at least my achievable dream car; there is no way I could afford an Aston Martin). So I went out and bought it—an Infinity G35. I talked myself into it because, after all, I was single and didn't have a family or debt. But guess what? After three months, I was disappointed to realize that my G35 was, well, just a car. Plus, every time a rock cracked my windshield, I wished I had a cheaper behicle so I wouldn't have to pay to replace it and continue maintaining the look of my nice car. (Am I the only one who does stuff like this?)

For you, it may not be a car. It may be your relationships, your job, or some kind of addiction; but we all make choices in the hopes that they'll make us happy.

What are you counting on right now to make you happy?

What's one decision you made recently thinking it would make you happier?

Wanting to be happy in and of itself is not a problem. But what happens when a scheme to become happy fails us? What happens when we're disappointed? What happens when we're wounded by the very thing we thought would make us happy?

When our dreams don't come true, we can become disillusioned. Depending on how we deal with that disillusionment, we can become cynical. Cynicism, over time, makes us jaded. And once we've become jaded, we refuse to invest ourselves in life, and we're left with only despair. I have seen this cycle over and over again. Most of the time, we get stuck in cynicism. But there are some things we can do to move out of the cycle and into hope:

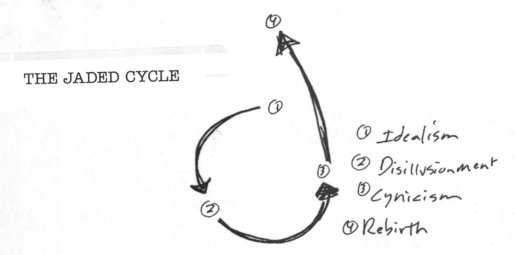

THE JADED CYCLE

① Idealism
② Disillusionment
③ Cynicism
④ Rebirth

HURTING OURSELVES

Let's look at God's example. Through His commitment to a relationship with humanity, He has opened Himself up to every possibility of disappointment. Throughout history, God has revealed His heart as He called people to serve Him. But from the beginning they turned their backs on Him. In Genesis, we see that God created this world as a good place for people to live in relationship with Him. But humanity, starting with Adam and Eve, turned away.

When Adam and Eve chose to disobey God, they brought pain into the world. Pain is an innate consequence of sin. I used to think the consequences of sin were either given out directly by God as He zapped us when we did bad things or they were saved up until God could beat us over the head with them after we were dead. It was one of my greatest fears as a kid—that God would show all my worst stuff on an enormous TV screen in heaven. (In fact, they actually showed a video about that in my youth group. Talk about frightening!) But that version of what happens when we sin is not exactly accurate.

God is not sitting up in heaven waiting to zap us for the bad stuff we do, but the effects of our bad choices *do cause* a lot of pain. When we go against God's plan for our lives and the world, we hurt ourselves by the very choices we make. Even when people seem to "get away" with doing wrong, they aren't actually getting away with anything. Sin brings pain to us and those around us sooner or later.

Think of a time when someone let you down. What was that like?

How do you think God may have felt when Adam and Eve deliberately turned against Him in the garden of Eden?

Think about a time when you disregarded God in your own life. How did He respond to you?

What pain have you experienced because of a choice to turn away from God?

The Bible doesn't use emotional language to describe God's reaction after Adam and Eve's choice, but it does record His response to their sin. God moved His people out of the garden and into the wild to live out the effects of their choices.

The consequences of Adam and Eve's decision were disastrous. The new world that God created—which was very good—was broken. Perfect order was replaced with a sort of controlled chaos as everything right down to the animals, plants, and mountains felt the effects of their sin. It was as if God's great and beautiful masterpiece was suddenly marred by a stain that ultimately infiltrated every part.

In choosing to sin, Adam and Eve gave up their claim to eternal life and unbroken fellowship with God. Their lives were flipped upside down. The blessing became the curse; the work became the toil; the fellowship became the banishment. But there is an interesting detail in Genesis 3 that gives us more insight into the complex emotions of God. Even though humanity willfully, blatantly, and consciously chose to go against God resulting in catastrophe we find God doing something more than punishing Adam and Eve:

"The Lord God made clothing out of skins for Adam and his wife, and He clothed them" (Genesis 3:21).

At the same time He was handing out discipline, God took time to provide for a seemingly insignificant need for those He loved—He covered their nakedness, thereby helping them deal with their shame.

It seems as though He is always doing things like that, doesn't it? Even when God is disciplining us, He is always thinking about our future. You could even go so far as to say that God never disciplines His children without including some element of redemption. God had a choice: He could abandon the world He had created, or He could salvage it. He chose—and still chooses—to engage with people even when they hurt Him through their disobedience. He doesn't give up; He still moves forward.

WHAT ABOUT US?

It's easy to become disillusioned when we face the fact that life is far from perfect. The effects of sin ripple throughout our world and into our lives. Things won't always turn out the way we want them to. We have hopes, and we face failures. We become wounded, then cynical, then jaded. So many people I know struggle with a jaded cynicism—including me.

Yet it's incredible to know that we have a God who is working to bring healing and hope to our world, and He will not rest until He does so.

In each session in this study, we will look at one element of the cycle that can make us jaded. I hope that you will find some freshness and renewal at the end. If we are willing to choose the kind of life that Jesus wants for us, then we don't have to be dominated by disappointment. We can instead escape from the jaded cycle and start living with a sense of hope. I don't pretend to have all the answers, but I have come to a place of renewal in some areas of my life. I believe that learning how to pass from despair to hope is necessary for everyone since we all have at least a little hands-on knowledge about despair.

If you're serious about breaking the cycle in your life, you must first decide how badly you want to do so. Before we go any further, commit to be honest with yourself as you work through this study. If you don't make this decision beforehand, it will be hard to follow through. This is a choice to look at the dark, hidden places of your life. It will be difficult, but it will be worth it.

I hope today will be the beginning of healing for you. At the end of this study, you may have even more questions than you started with, but every search for truth begins with questions. And often, the willingness to ask the questions can take us deeper in our walk with Jesus. My hope is that you will find a new quest, one that leads to hope and joy in Jesus Christ. You are at the beginning of an exciting journey.

BEFORE YOU START THE STUDY, PLEASE SPEND 15 MINUTES (OR MORE) SITTING BEFORE GOD ASKING HIM TO REVEAL WHAT'S AT THE TOP OF HIS PLAN FOR YOUR LIFE. USE THIS TIME TO OPEN YOURSELF TO HEARING FROM HIM.

SESSION ONE

Idealism

EVERYONE I KNOW HAS HIS OR HER OWN EXPECTATIONS OF HOW LIFE SHOULD
turn out. But I may be the worst when it comes to this. For one thing, it's how I'm wired. I am constantly trying to figure out the future. I think part of my personality requires that I regularly make lists and get things done. But it's also a family trait.

Every time my extended family gets together for the holidays or vacation, we share our dreams for the next five years. We share where we see God leading us and what new developments we see coming. We love to dream about what could be; it's a great part of our heritage. It's also a difficult thing to balance.

There's nothing wrong with dreams in and of themselves; idealism is something rooted in our hearts as God's creation. The issue is more about the way we dream and hope for the world around us.

The problem is this: When my dreams don't come true, I grow discouraged.

For any of us, when our idealistic dreams don't come true, it can be tempting to disengage from the world and people around us in order to avoid being hurt again. If left unguarded, our idealism ironically becomes the first step to cynicism.

THE WAY IT SHOULD BE

I define *idealism* as an emotional belief in the way things could be and should be. The reason for the phrase *emotional belief* is that our ideals are more than simple expectations. We get excited when talk about our dreams. Our hearts start to pound, and our voices rise. The point is we have an emotional response when we think hopefully about the future. Then, if our ideal scenarios don't play themselves out, we are deeply affected. Frustrated. Disappointed. Disillusioned.

Idealistic people believe that the world, or at least their world, should work a certain way. For some, they think things should run perfectly. No one should ever be sick. People shouldn't let them down. They should have perfectly healthy relationships and all the money they need. Not only *could* it be that way—it *should* be.

It's easy to fall into this category, especially as Christians in an affluent society. We tend to believe that it is our "right" as human beings and definitely as Christ-followers to receive good things. We should have good health. We should have lights and running water. We definitely should be without pain, and when those things don't happen, it seems as though something is wrong. We can begin to think it's God's fault because we trusted Him for the good things that didn't materialize.

> How would you describe your idealistic expectations for your life? What about for the world?

> Are you a big goal-setter? What goals have you made recently?

REALITY CHECK

All of us are idealistic in one way or another. We have ideas about how the world should work—a best-case scenario. We think our parents should be supportive and compassionate. They should love each other well. Our careers should take off, and our relationships with managers and co-workers should be professional and positive. Our love lives should be right out of a chick flick. The person we are with should be both attractive and attentive to us. Our church leaders should be kind and pure. Our churches should be welcoming places for outsiders and should be championing the causes of the poor.

We can romanticize life to the extent that reality can never keep up. I get frustrated at my own heart for buying into this kind of idealism. It only leads to discontentedness. If I let it go unchecked, it leads to a lifestyle where life is all about what I want.

Let me repeat, idealism in and of itself is not bad. But when all my ideals begin to revolve around me in an unrealistic way, then my idealism becomes an unguarded monster. The danger is that this self-centered monster disengages from reality and often inflicts pain on others.

Idealism is where the jaded cycle begins. The whole cycle can be headed off if we can redirect ourselves at the idealism stage. We need a clear understanding of the expectations we have about the quality of our day-to-day experiences. Take a look at the cycle one more time.

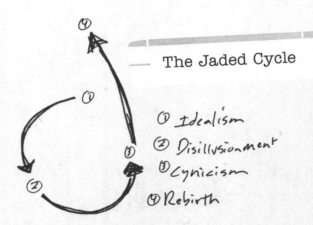

The Jaded Cycle

① Idealism
② Disillusionment
③ Cynicism
④ Rebirth

When idealism rules our lives, it is impossible to focus on others. We begin to believe the lie that the whole world is really the stage for our live performances. It feels as though we are caught in some sort of drama starring ourselves. In that movie, we are the star; everyone else is just a supporting character. What matters is what we want, what we feel, and what we think. Anything that detracts from our idea of how the story should unfold is a threat that could derail the entire plot.

In *Blue Like Jazz,* Donald Miller suggests that we all essentially star in the movie of our lives. Check out the book for further discussion of the implications that self-centeredness brings to our relationships with others.

How have any of your dreams or ideals set you up for disappointment?

Most of us tend to feel like the world revolves around us until some kind of disappointment—or worse, a wound—interrupts our lives. How do we guard ourselves emotionally in a healthy way? We need to be able to hope and dream, but we need to do so inside of the real world. So how can we retain the purity of hope while living in reality? We have to protect our hearts both from the outside and the inside.

PROTECT YOUR HEART

First, we can guard our hearts from outside things that may corrupt us. That might sound old-fashioned, but the truth is we have to be careful what we expose ourselves to if we want to make sure that we keep our souls healthy.

In Western culture we face many obstacles to healthy hearts. To begin with, we are driven by consumerism. Businesses that want to sell us something do their best to cultivate some level of discontent in us. At its core, the purpose of advertising is to make us feel like we need something else—something more—whether we do or not. The message is loud and clear: "The more you have, the happier you will become." I have bought into that lie more times than I can count. But Jesus asked what good it does us to gain the whole world—every new latest and greatest thing—and lose our own souls (Luke 9:25).

In addition to recognizing our consumeristic tendencies, approaching our relationships in a healthy way can give us a measure of protection. We have to find ways to keep our expectations realistic especially regarding how we'll be fulfilled through other people. The reality is, no person or relationship can offer us wholeness or happiness. God is the only One who can meet us in the deepest places of our hearts.

My friend Emily has taken drastic measures in this area. She has decided not to watch romantic movies because she does not want to define romance unrealistically. She realizes that if she begins to project the behavior of the guy from *The Notebook* onto her husband, then she will be dissatisfied with their relationship. She knows that it's unfair to hold real-world relationships to the standard of a bunch of famous actors following a movie script.

"Guard your heart above all else, for it is the source of life" (Proverbs 4:23).

To combat "church-hopping," Joshua Harris wrote the book *Stop Dating the Church*. Consider it as a further resource if your cynicism has prevented you from planting deep roots in a fellowship of Christ-followers.

Most of us buy into the lies of our culture, though. We jump from relationship to relationship because someone doesn't fit our expectations. Similarly, we believe we need a new car because ours is showing a little wear. We move from job to job or from church to church, always looking for the *right* thing—the ideal.

When discontentment and cynicism rise up in our hearts, we lose the joy in life. Our hearts become divided, and we grieve the heart of God. He only wants to help us become who be who He created to be—not who we think we should make ourselves into so that we can be happy.

What sort of things do you need to protect yourself from?

In which areas do you think you may not be guarding your heart enough?

STAY ALERT

There is something bigger going on in the world and our lives than just these things. At the root of all our temptations there is a spiritual conflict raging. Peter wanted to impress this reality on the readers of his first letter.

He wrote to believers who were spread throughout the part of the world we now call Turkey. The people there were new believers who were experiencing religious persecution. Peter advised them how to live in the midst of turmoil. If you pay attention, you'll see that Peter defines every problem they are facing in a spiritual light. He tells them to be aware of their circumstances, to open their eyes to the true source of their danger:

**"Be sober! Be on the alert! Your adversary the Devil is prowling around like a roaring lion, looking for anyone he can devour"
(1 Peter 5:8).**

The Chistains during Peter's day were persecuted because they were seen as a threat to the social structure. It was the accepted practice of the time for each of the peoples who had been conquered by the Roman empire to offer sacrifices to their god on behalf of the Roman emperor. Christians—since they believed Jesus was the last and ultimate sacrifice— did not offer sacrifices at all, much less on on behalf of the emperor.

We need to know who our enemy is. In the movie *The Usual Suspects,* Kevin Spacey's character tells the investigating detective that the greatest trick the devil ever pulled off was to make the world believe that he didn't exist. Maybe the first step of defense is to realize that you are being attacked. If you read just a little of the Bible, you will see spiritual forces at work constantly.

Often we think that temptation is strictly about the object of temptation. But our battle is not just about food, materialism, lust, or cynicism—it's more spiritual than that:

"For our battle is not against flesh and blood, but against the rulers, against the authorities, against the world powers of this darkness, against the spiritual forces of evil in the heavens" (Ephesians 6:12).

What evidence do you see of the enemy's work in the world?

Make two columns. In one column write down three things the Bible says about Satan. In the other column write down three things our popular culture and media communicates about Satan. Compare your list with the rest of the group.

PRIDE GOES BEFORE THE FALL

One of the key attributes of our spiritual enemy is pride. We can learn a lot about him from the Old Testament prophet Ezekiel.

Read Ezekiel 28:11-19.

Many Bible translations have a heading for this section reading something like "A Lament for Tyre's King." Tyre was the capital of the kingdom of the Phoenicians, a powerful, ancient people group known for their sailing ability and world travel. But according to Ezekiel, there was something else at work behind the Phonecians.

Throughout the Bible there is the understanding that all warfare for Israel has a spiritual undertone. You see this in the famous ten plagues of Egypt (Exodus 7–12). You might not know it, but those plagues actually target the various gods of Egypt. You can also see this perspective of warfare with spiritual undertones throughout Hebrew poetry.

At the beginning of chapter 28, Ezekiel prophesied about the downfall of the actual human ruler of Tyre and of Pheonicia. But in verses 11-19, he lamented the loss of the true king of Tyre, Satan. The prophet pointed to him as the real power behind the throne.

The language and imagery indicate that this is no longer a human Ezekiel is writing about. This king is said to have been in Eden and was covered in precious stones; however, this being fell from grace because of his sin—his own pride. Verse 17 says that this ruler's heart became proud because of his own beauty, and he corrupted his wisdom because of his desire for his own splendor. Basically, Satan began to seek his own glory and set himself against God.

We don't actually know the true name of the being we call Satan. The word *Satan* is from the Greek work, *o'satanas,* which means "adversary" or "enemy." It is a descriptive name, but it's not a proper name like Steve or Shelly. Many people would say that his name is Lucifer, or "light bearer," but that is only the name coined by the scholar Jerome when he was translating the phrase "son of the dawn, son of the morning" in Isaiah.

The name of God's enemy lies lost in time. Meanwhile, the name of Jesus is the most known in the entire world, and His name will be held above that of every name (Philippians 2:10-11). Satan's pride demanded that another name besides that of Jesus take a place of glory in universal history, and that pride was ultimately his undoing.

Three thoughts strike me when considering Satan.

1. God lamented His loss. In verse 12 God called Ezekiel to lament over this loss and the ensuing wickedness. God will someday utterly destroy Satan, and even though the end is in sight for this enemy of God, he is still mourned.

When delivering the children of Israel from slavery in Exodus 7-12, God chose specific wonders to perform as a display of His power. Among other things, God turned the Nile to blood and caused darkness to fall over the land. All the plagues corresponded to a god that the Egyptians worshiped. By choosing to perform these specific wonders, God not only delivered His people, but He also proved His dominance over the gods of the Egyptians.

For a deeper perspective on Satan and his tactics, read *The Screwtape Letters,* C.S. Lewis' classic work of fiction concerning spiritual warfare.

2. Satan wants to devour and destroy us. There is no good left in him. He is not here just to give us a bad day or to kill some of our joy. He wants to utterly destroy us and leave us with nothing.

3. God is vastly greater than Satan. In Ezekiel 28:18-19, as well as Revelation 20, it is prophesied that Satan will be destroyed forever. He is not free to do everything he wants; he has not gained independence from God. The moral of the story is this: Don't fear Satan more than God.

It's important to understand that even though there's an enemy out to destroy you, he can be resisted. To be alert and sober (1 Peter 5:8) means to keep your head up and not be caught off guard. The way to combat Satan is to stand firm in the faith, to resist him. Stay strong in what you believe. Hold onto the fact that God already has the ultimate victory, and He has your back.

> List some things you are struggling with right now, and see if you can identify a spiritual component at work. Take a moment to pray for God's insight into your struggle.

> What are some specific ways to "stand firm" in your faith?

THE PRIDE CONNECTION

So what's the connection to the jaded cycle? Idealism can be a form of pride, which is not of God. That's why we have to guard our idealistic hearts.

Prideful idealism claims that we know how the world should be run. So when the world doesn't run that way and our expectations about life aren't fulfilled, we often stumble into disillusionment and cynicism.

So how do we keep ourselves from prideful idealism? We can start by spending time asking God to change our hearts. When we try and try exclusively by our willpower to change our character we neglect the most important part of spiritual development—reliance on the Holy Spirit. It's with His help, that character change is possible.

> **Take a moment to ask the Holy Spirit help you overcome pride in your life. The first step to humility is to ask for God's help, so go for it. Write your prayer here:**

One of the most practical ways you can combat prideful idealism is to learn to submit to the godly leadership in your life. Peter told his young male readers to "be subject to the elders" (1 Peter 5:5). This passage doesn't just apply to younger men but to all of us who are under authority.

Of course, that's not so easy. I often think I have better ideas than some of my leaders. But what I have learned is that people with more life experience often make wiser decisions. So if you want to learn humility, learn how to wait for your leadership and submit to wise counsel.

Submitting yourself to the leadership of the people God has placed in your life—bosses, teachers, parents, pastors—doesn't mean you become a mindless clone. But it does mean you support them, and that takes humility, especially when you disagree with them.

Peter says to *clothe* ourselves with humility (1 Peter 5:5). This poetic language asks us to cover ourselves in humility—to let it protect and shield us. Here are two tips on how to be humble under authority:

1. Support your authorities publicly. That may sound simple, but start small. Little action steps result in big change. For example, verbally support your boss to your co-workers. That doesn't make you a brown-noser. Your boss needs to know you believe in him or her. It's really hard to lead people when you feel like no one will get behind you. I have learned that loyalty in public leads to

The word *submit* is made from the compound of the Greek words for "under" and "to order." Therefore, to submit is to place in an orderly fashion under something. Because the word is applied to men, women, and even Jesus in Scripture, it does not imply lesser importance, but simply an order to be maintained.

influence in private. I am more likely to listen to the people who I know are my public supporters. Support your leader in meetings and then if you have any suggestions, talk to him or her later when he or she is more likely to listen.

2. Use the right channels to effect change. This is extremely hard for me because I'm a rebel at heart. Can you relate? I have found the best way to implement my "great new ideas" is to use the established power channels and processes. Dreaming about what could be and should be is a good thing, but when you start going above or around your authority, your idea will probably be dismissed. Rules usually exist to keep your organization from total chaos, so don't try to reinvent the wheel on your own.

As you might have guessed, I'm sharing this because of a mistake I made. There was a ministry that I thought could be run much better. I thought I had the solution no one else had. So one day, when my boss's boss asked my opinion, I gave it to him without any mercy. I didn't realize until later that my comments had unknowingly thrown both my boss and his boss under the bus. In my pride, I had forgotten to honor my leaders, and I looked like a fool as a result—serious low point. After licking my wounds for a couple of weeks, I made a conscious choice to bring about change within a structure the right way. This has been one of my wisest decisions.

If you dare, look inside and ask yourself in which ways you may be resisting authority. Maybe you're resentful of a boss or your spiritual leaders. Maybe you defy them behind their backs. That kind of rebellion is often not rooted in a desire for good, but pride. These are your red flags are a good moment to check your own motives and remind you to humble yourself before God. Surrender to Him the way you think things should be.

> **Write out a struggle with leadership you are dealing with right now. What specific steps could you take to make a decision to honor authority?**

TIMING REALLY IS EVERYTHING

We unguarded idealists can become viciously committed to our own agendas and our own timing. We want to make it happen and make it happen now! Letting go of both agendas and timing requires the humility we've already talked about. First Peter 5:6-7 says that we need to wait on God by following these instructions:

"Humble yourselves therefore under the mighty hand of God, so that He may exalt you in due time, casting all your cares upon Him because He cares about you."

It's important to be willing to wait for the right time for our dreams to come true. That is what we learn in 1 Peter 5:6—when we cast our cares on God, He will lift us up *when the time is right*. Humble trust in God allows us to breathe while we are waiting.

> What dream do you need to wait on? What should you say "no" to as a way of humbly trusting in God's timing?

The lesson of waiting for God's timing was one the disciple learned with some difficulty. Throughout the Gospels he was considered to be hot-headed, impetuous, and even violent at times (see Mark 9:5-6; Matthew 26:31-35; and Matthew 26:50-54 for some examples).

What would our lives look like if we were more humble? We would trust God and probably see Him working more in our lives. We would keep ourselves from a lot of unnecessary pain and wounds when things don't turn out the way we had hoped. But most importantly, we would find hope that Jesus is working in and through us no matter how our circumstances seem to be turning out at the moment. I encourage you to dream in humility. To dream humbly is to embrace the vision that God has for your life. It is to trust Him to make it happen—or not—at the right time.

Breaking the Cycle

O Write a personal note to someone in authority over you. Let him or her know of your support and appreciation.

O Take inventory of your schedule. Evaluate each activity based on whether it lines up with your agenda or God's.

O Each week your group leader will make suggestions about how you can connect with your group outside of your scheduled meeting time. Take advantage of that opportunity.

"GOD, BRILLIANT LORD,
YOURS IS A HOUSEHOLD NAME.
NURSING INFANTS GURGLE
CHORUSES ABOUT YOU;
TODDLERS SHOUT THE SONGS
THAT DROWN OUT ENEMY TALK,
AND SILENCE ATHEIST BABBLE.
I LOOK UP AT YOUR MACRO-SKIES,
DARK AND ENORMOUS,
YOUR HANDMADE SKY-JEWELRY,
MOON AND STARS MOUNTED
IN THEIR SETTINGS.
THEN I LOOK AT MY MICRO-SELF AND
WONDER, WHY DO YOU BOTHER WITH US?
WHY TAKE A SECOND LOOK OUR WAY?"

PSALM 8:1-5, THE MESSAGE

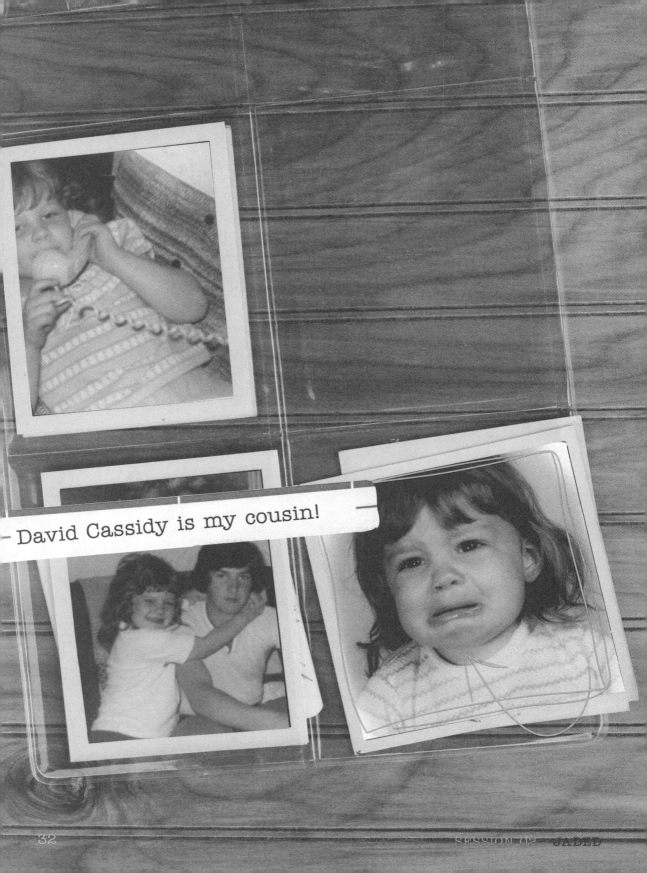

David Cassidy is my cousin!

SESSION TWO

The Wounding

I HATE GETTING HURT. I hate it most when I don't see it coming.

Last summer a bunch of my close friends planned a canoe trip down the Spring River in northern Arkansas. Three of us decided to leave early and go spelunking in some caves in the area first. This was one of those adventures we thought we could just figure out as we went, so we didn't bother to find out exactly where the caves were. Turns out, they were 75 miles away. So our adventurous caving expedition turned into a trip to the local Sonic.

On the way back to our cabin, we wanted to go off-roading in the Jeep Wrangler with the top down. We started looking for an unpaved path to explore or some power lines to follow. Alan, who was driving, spotted a road back into the woods, so we turned around to take a closer look. That's when the "incident" happened.

Keep in mind that Jeeps are top heavy, and we may or nay not have been driving a little too fast. As Alan made his turn, we began to lose contact with the pavement. The Jeep flipped onto its side and skidded to a stop in the middle of the road. I was riding in the back seat, and (idiotically) I didn't have on my seat belt. As the Jeep started to flip, I grabbed the nearest seat belt with both fists and white-knuckled it for dear life. I still fell on the roll bar.

We lay there in shock for a couple of minutes before we started laughing, amazed we were still alive. And while the other guys were fine, my back was hurting. After we flipped the Jeep back over, it started (unbelievably), so we headed to the hospital to find out if I was OK. On the way, thoughts started flashing through my head: *Am I going to be paralyzed? Will I be wounded for life? What's going to happen to me?*

A FACT OF LIFE

We ended up at a small hospital, where we were told we'd have to wait for the doctor to "come back from supper" before he could diagnose what was wrong. By then, the pain was pretty intense. When the doctor checked me out, though, the diagnosis was too good to be true: I hadn't broken my spine; I had only sprained several muscles in my back. Still, I'd have to stay immobile for the next couple of weeks to heal.

I hobbled away with the following conclusions:
1. Getting hurt usually comes when we least expect it.
2. Pain is a huge inconvenience, and recovery takes a long time.
3. Riding in a vehicle sans seat belt is not advisable.

Unfortunately, we all have wounding moments in our lives. These wounds can be spiritual, physical, relational, emotional, or mental. Occasionally the wounds are so painful that they define who we are, and we live the rest of our lives in light of that experience. We can eventually become prisoners to our past because every time the memory comes back, we instantly feel pain and react negatively. We can begin to act as victims instead of healthy people.

Of course, everyone's wounds are different, but these are a few wound-inflicting circumstances that are common:

- Maybe your parents divorced, and you felt betrayed. How could two people who said that they loved each other and committed themselves for life split up? As a result, you may even doubt that marriage can really ever work. You may distrust relationships, and at some level wonder if God is real because He allowed it to happen.

- Maybe you are the person who divorced. You thought you had found true love, and then your spouse left or cheated or "conveniently" fell out of love. Now you are wondering what the point of it all was. You're sure you don't want to trust anyone again.

- Maybe you were someone who trusted a person of authority in the church, like a youth pastor or Bible study leader. In your eyes that person was everything a Christian is supposed to be, but he or she let you down. That "ideal" person stole some money, had an affair, were hurtful toward you, or blew you off. Now you struggle with your faith because if God is real, why are His followers such terrible examples?

If you've ever thought that things in the world, your family, or your life are not as they should be, you're not alone. Philip Yancey examines this issue further in his book *Disappointment with God*.

- Maybe you've been wounded by your job. You thought that things would work out differently in your career. You expected to rise to the top of the organization easily. But now, you hate to go to work. It just seems like a dead-end. You aren't satisfied anymore, and you dislike your boss and your coworkers.

- Maybe you have lost a child or a loved one to some terrible tragedy. Maybe you have been physically sick for a long time, and you are exhausted. You just wish you could get past it, but it's ridiculously difficult. You may feel that no one understands. You may feel helpless.

- Maybe you're sick and tired of the injustice in the world. You hear people talking about doing good for others, but their lives don't match their words. You wonder why AIDS is ravaging so much of the African continent, how children can be sold into prostitution, and why millions of people starve or die of easily preventable diseases, while wealthy people around the world stand by and do nothing. You feel angry and may have shut down. You've become critical of people, but you don't have the energy to engage in your community.

> **If you resonate with any of this, go ahead and name the situation that has wounded or is wounding you. Share with your group if you choose to. Naming your wound is a first step toward healing. (Don't be surprised if it's hard or emotional for you to share.)**

Throughout your experience with *Jaded*, you will have opportunities to listen to a roundtable discussion with some young adults of differing backgrounds, opinions, and professions. They will be discussing some of the same ideas that *Jaded* is based on.

Listen to "The Hope and the Healing—Part I." Your leader will send it to you via e-mail.

If you have been wounded, you're probably tired of all the religious-speak—people telling you there is a reason behind it all and that God has a purpose. It's easy to think, *God, if You are out there, why don't You just fix this stuff? Or at least let me know the purpose because this hurts too much.*

It's OK to feel that way. It really is. This is real life. Terrible stuff happens to people, and life is hard.

If you haven't experienced a deep wound yet, you are fortunate, but it will probably happen to you if you're engaged in life. It's not being jaded to admit that pain is a fact of life and that the world we live in is a broken place because of sin. What is jaded is to freeze up and refuse to continue fully living. In the Bible, God gives us a record of people who have wrestled with loss, disappointment, and pain. These narratives are great case studies about how to move past our own wounds.

> **Think about people in the Bible who were wounded. List some of their stories. How did they deal with their pain? What about people in our world today? How are they dealing with pain?**

Most of the time we become wounded when our expectations about how life could and should be fail us. At that point, it's easy to "toughen up" and withdraw into cynicism so that we won't be hurt again.

> **How have you typically responded to wounding in your life?**

Throughout Scripture, God used the analogy of marriage to illustrate His relationship to Israel, and later, the church. Marriage is meant to be the most intimate, honest, and vulnerable of relationships, indicating the kind of relationship God desires to have with His people.

> **Think about times when you've withdrawn. Who did you pull away from? What was the reason?**

As you continue to study the jaded cycle, you'll see that one thing leads to another. After you're wounded, you can fall prey to a variety of negative emotions if you don't check yourself and choose to move past your pain.

A WOUNDED GOD?

The Bible talks about many ancients who were wounded by both the people they trusted as friends as well as by those they considered to be enemies. But God has been the Being who has been the most offended and hurt of anyone throughout the biblical record.

Every sin His people indulge in is a personal offense to Him. Every lie, act of greed, or lustful thought is a slap in the face of His perfect character. Sin brings separation between God and His creation. Yet He still continues to engage us and fight for connectedness. It's amazing to see Him continue to battle for our hearts when we so often reject Him with our actions.

A look at history shows how God specifically chose to reveal Himself to the Jewish nation. He chose them and raised them out of nothing. If you study God's relationship with these people, you'll see Him asking them to obey rules that He laid down for their own good. What God really wanted, though, more than mere obedience was a relationship in which they would love and worship Him alone.

Unfortunately, the Israelites consistently chose to worship the gods of their surrounding neighbors rather than the one true God. Maybe it was because trying something new is attractive and exciting. Maybe it's because it's in our nature as humans to choose a god we can personally control.

Even today, we find gods of our own that we choose over the living God. Some are not simply another world religion like Buddhism or Islam, but money, a love relationship, or even ourselves.

> Have you struggled with having a stronger loyalty to something or someone than you do to God? What were the first steps that led you there?

When you're struggling to cope in life and struggling to trust God to take care of you, what do you find yourself holding onto for balance?

Why is it so tempting to define your own terms for living instead of following God's direction?

God's relationship with His people is illustrated as a marriage in the Bible. Just to lighten the mood during this study, watch a marriage-themed comedy like *Meet the Parents* or *My Big, Fat Greek Wedding*.

LOOKING FOR A QUICK FIX

The people of Israel tended to pursue the gods of the neighboring nation, the Canaanites. These gods were not anything like the God of the Bible. Instead of being one Creator of everything, there were many different gods who supposedly did different things. The Canaanites' main god, however, was the sky god Baal. In their belief system, Baal functioned as a fertility god. That meant he was tied to the main source of their way of life—agriculture. They believed he was the one who provided the rain for the crops they ate, and in an agricultural society, there is nothing more important. Having water meant having life.

The Bible is not a G-rated book. If you read closely, you may be shocked to discover how graphic it is. Fertility religions are hardly the stuff that you want to tell small children about, but they were everywhere in biblical times. The goal of Baal worship was to get him to make it rain. In that fertility religion, they believed rain happened when Baal approached his female companion, Ashtoreth, and slept with her. So if you wanted to get the attention of a fertility god, it was pretty simple. You would go to the nearest Baal temple, and you would pay a "priest" or "priestess"—temple prostitutes—to have sex with you. That was the main mode of "worship."

Let's just say they didn't have a lot of attendance problems.

We don't do the Bible justice when we merely say these religions were detestable. These temples were incredibly offensive; outside them were signs of large phallic symbols called Ashtoreth poles. Yet God's people would leave their own God, the One who had rescued them time and time again, to go serve false idols that offered an immediate payoff of pleasure. Yep, this made God very angry.

> **Often we are tempted to abandon what we know is right for what will provide a more immediate payoff. Why do you think we do that?**

> **What drives us to look for a quick fix in the happiness department?**

God didn't see the Hebrews' disobedience as simple disloyalty, like some general who watched a soldier desert the army. He saw it as a lover whose bride cheated on him with his worst enemy. It was personal, and it was heart-breaking.

> **Write down the way you have felt when you were rejected by someone you loved. Do those feelings change your understanding of God's perspective?**

"You adulterous wife, who receives strangers instead of her husband! Men give gifts to all prostitutes, but you gave gifts to all your lovers. You bribed them to come to you from all around for your sexual favors" (Ezekiel 16:32-33).

Through the years, God used tough times to get His people's attention. When bad things happened to them, they would suddenly focus on God. When things were easy, they would slide back into the fertility religions, forgetting all about Him. It was an ongoing pattern of continuing in sin until they needed to be rescued.

Sound familiar? You may be dealing with something like this in your own life—most of us do at one time or another. When tough times hit, the prayers start going up. When we get caught in this cycle, we are wounding the heart of God. He wants all of our hearts, no matter what kind of circumstances we're facing in life.

HOSEA, THE PROPHET

In the Old Testament, God spoke to His people through prophets. They were pretty radical guys who heard God speak to them directly. At times, the instructions God gave them didn't seem to make much sense. Then, as the prophet followed those directives, his very life became an object lesson to get people's attention and bring their hearts back to God. (The books in the Old Testament that follow Song of Songs are the writings of these prophets.)

The prophet Hosea had a unique story. He lived after the kingdoms of David and Solomon when things were kind of winding down politically for the people of Israel. Their sin had led them into a downward spiral of national self-destruction.

Read Hosea 1:2-3.

Kind of amazing, isn't it? God told a prophet to go marry someone named Gomer—a woman who was promiscuous. It was safe to assume from her relational track record that she would not be a faithful wife.

Hosea's marriage was an image of the way God felt about the people of Israel. In verse 2, God told Hosea to do this because "the whole land has been promiscuous by abandoning the Lord." The marriage of Gomer and Hosea mirrored the relationship between God and His people. Gomer was operating as a prostitute even while she was married, just like the Israelites were worshiping other gods even while God was taking care of them.

God is not like you and me. He is willing to risk even though He has been injured. He pursues even when He is pushed aside. In a sense, He chooses to hope and also to provide hope for His people.

Read Hosea 3:1-5.

Incredibly, even after Gomer left Hosea for her old life, God told him to buy her back and restore her as his wife. By law, Hosea had the right to have her stoned to death for committing adultery, but instead he chose to re-connect and forgive her.

Hosea and Gomer had three children, two of whom quite possibly were illegitimate. The names of the kids were symbolic of Israel's disobedience. Hosea's entire life was a living illustration of Israel's ever-worsening relationship with God (Hosea 1:2-11).

Can you imagine what Gomer might have thought when Hosea showed up? *Oh no! I am going to die. He is going to kill me!* Imagine her surprise when instead he paid her release and took her home. She wasn't even worth the price of a slave. A slave was worth thirty pieces of silver, but she was worth fifteen silver pieces and five bushels of barley. Still, Hosea found value in her.

It's the same for us. God chooses to re-engage with us. Hosea's relationship with Gomer was a parallel of the relationship God had with His people Israel. Even though they turned their backs against Him and chose to follow false gods, He chose to redeem them and bring them back.

A MESSY PROCESS

The process God used to bring His faithless bride back to Himself was an incredibly painful one. It was a defining event in the Old Testament that marked God's people from that point forward. Hosea prophesied about it:

"For the Israelites must live many days without king or prince, without sacrifice or sacred pillars, and without ephod or household idols. Afterwards, the people of Israel will return and seek the LORD their God and David their king" (Hosea 3:4-5a).

What happened? A wounded God inflicted a wound on His people. On their way back from squashing the Egyptian empire, King Nebuchadnezzar and the fierce warriors of Babylon defeated the Jewish army and physically exiled the Jews, deporting them to different parts of the world.

Can you imagine if someone came to your city or town and took everyone away to somewhere on the other side of the world? Imagine the huge culture shock. Not only would you not know the language, but suddenly you would not have any rights or relational connections. You might start wondering if God was really with you or if He existed at all. Talk about being wounded.

> When you are wounded, how does it affect your perception of God?

Though there are several exiles recorded in the history of the Israelites, the most devastating came at the hands of the Babylonians in 586 B.C. After a six-month siege on the city of Jerusalem, the Babylonians breached the walls, destroyed the temple, confiscated its treasures, and took the survivors into captivity.

God was wounded by the unfaithfulness of His people. His people were wounded by the consequences of their own sin. It's important to recognize that God did not act in revenge. When He chose for His people to be wounded, He did so with the hope that they would return to Him. His people had a choice about how they would respond to the wound, and so do we.

Whether we are wounded by someone we've trusted, or whether we bring the wounding on ourselves, we still have to be careful how we respond to pain. Will we withdraw? Will we let our disillusionment lead us to cynicism? Will we continue to engage life and let God renew us?

Listen to "Jaded" by LaRue on your playlist. Do the lyrics strike a chord of truth about your own life?

A CONNECTING PAIN

However you've been wounded, remember that even though there is tremendous pain now, you are still involved in God's process. It's easy to forget this in the midst of struggle. Maybe we don't want to believe it. Maybe the pain is just too intense. There is a temptation to let our wounds define us, but that is never healthy. C.S. Lewis once said that "God whispers to us in our pleasure, speaks in our conscience, but shouts in our pains: It is his megaphone to rouse a deaf world."

Your pain may actually be something God uses to reconnect with you. He may be trying to wake you up like He did the Israelites. Pain is not pleasant, but it does have value and purpose in the plan of God.

In what ways could God be using your wounds to wake you up?

How do you typically hear or perceive God speaking to you?

So how should we respond when life deals us a painful blow? Do we just grin and take it and say that God has a reason for everything? That isn't good enough for me, and I'm thinking it isn't good enough for you either. That response requires at least a little bit of inauthenticity. Still, there are some practical ways to respond in a healthy way to wounding.

WHAT DEFINES YOU?

Many people I know walk around interpreting their lives in light of their wounds. I know several people who have allowed their relationship with their father, or the non-relationship, to define their lives. Women often enter unhealthy relationships as a result of trying to get their father needs met by someone else. Men often live their lives trying to prove that they can earn enough, win enough, or be enough for their father's approval. In each case, their wound only leaves them feeling more empty, and the cycle worsens.

Other friends were wounded at a church or by a religious leader. Now they use that as an excuse not to re-engage with God. They avoid church. It's not that they've become bad people. They may still call themselves Christians, but they are now unchurched. They still live in pain because they're allowing pain to define them instead of processing through it. They disengage from spirituality rather than face the wound that sent them reeling in the first place.

The only way out is to refuse to let a wound define you. Find something else to define you. If you don't, bitterness will swallow you whole and leave you disenfranchised at every level of your life.

THE TRUTH ABOUT WOUNDS

Receiving a wound is a hundred percent certainty for everyone who lives in this fallen world. Your wound may scar you for the rest of your life, but don't let that deter you from moving past it.

I remember taking a pretty bad fall off a ladder a couple of years ago. I wasn't that high off the ground—only about eight feet. I was taking down some signs when the ladder buckled beneath me and collapsed. All I knew was that one minute I was up minding my own business, and the next I was flying through the air. The only thought going through my head was, *This is going to be bad!*

Instead of landing on the floor, which was a hard enough landing place, I landed on the ladder, which was a worse option. People appeared out of nowhere when they heard my crash and asked the age-old, dumbest question possible: "Are you OK?" Seriously, I just fell off a ladder: I am probably not OK. "Where are you bleeding?" would have been a much more appropriate question.

I thought I was fine because all my arms and legs were still attached. Then I looked at my shin and realized why it felt like someone had hit me with a hammer halfway between my knee and my foot. I had a gash about an inch and a half long, and it went straight to the bone. I know this because I had never seen my tibia before, but there it was, gleaming in the sunshine. So someone raced me to the hospital to sit forever in the ER until a doctor could take care of me. He gave me six staples, and my leg looked really nasty for a while, but eventually I healed.

Here's my point: My life revolved around that wound for about two weeks. I couldn't lift anything heavy. The staples got caught on stuff. It was inconvenient to say the least, but eventually it went away. My wound became a scar, and what had once been trying and difficult became nothing more than another mark on my body. My wound no longer defines me or my actions. Unfortunately, emotional wounds take much longer to heal. But even in that healing process, we can make choices to be defined by something other than what hurts.

What wound are you tempted to let define you?

Imagine a time in the future when your wound is fully healed. Describe how your life would be different.

Many wounds are deep enough to warrant more discussion than your small group can provide. The American Association of Christian Counselors is a nationwide coalition of counselors who operate from a Christian perspective. To locate a counselor, visit *aacc.net*.

WHAT'S HURTING YOU?

They say that time heals all wounds, and I believe that's true. However, you can't move past your wounds until you identify them. A way to keep your wound from defining you is to call it by name and be willing to explore it. You may actually be acting out of pain in your life and not even know the cause of your anguish. The wound itself may be even deeper than your most recent painful event. If you're having trouble pinpointing it, consider finding some help. There may be someone you trust in your group or at your church you can talk to. You might want to talk to a trained counselor who can help you deal with your pain. If you do have something you are working through, please don't hesitate to talk it through with someone. Knowing is the first step to healing.

> What makes most people afraid to look inside their own pain? How about you? What holds you back from exploring your wounds?

Many people have wounds that are fairly minor, yet they still become bitter and cynical and begin to disconnect from God and people. Others have much more serious wounds that drive them to numb out pain by more desperate means. You may be one of those people who really struggle under the weight of your pain. If you aren't sure whether you're dealing with it well, you might want to ask close friends for their point of view.

Some of the signs that you may need help coping include consistent overspending; compulsively buying things you can't afford or don't need; sleeping too much (more than ten hours a day); or addictions to things like alcohol, sex, gambling, or narcotics. These are all coping mechanisms that commonly occur in people who are struggling to cope with major life wounds. If that's the case with you, I really encourage you to talk to a minister or counselor who has the tools to help you.

After being wounded, it's difficult to put yourself back out there again, to engage with people and take risks in life, but give it one more shot.

In what ways are you hesitant to risk opening up to people?

Why is it so difficult to put yourself back out there into life again after having been wounded?

What is the worst thing that could happen if you risk again? What could happen if you don't?

KEEP LIVING

We can't be afraid of pain to the point that we quit risking. Not to be pessimistic, but we will all be wounded regardless of whether we risk or not. That is normal life. However, God can use our wounds to advance His purposes and become more intimately connected to us. God reveals Himself through our wounds because it is through those experiences that He can be seen most clearly.

I often have a tendency to hold back just a little bit because I don't want to get hurt. I can tell you that will never get you anywhere. In college I really wanted to dunk a basketball, but as much as I tried, I couldn't quite get there. Then one day, I could. It was weird; I just went up and dunked the ball. Stunned, I did it again and again. It was so cool.

About thirty minutes later, I could hardly walk. I had pulled a muscle in my leg just above my knee. The strain had been too much. My doctor told me that I couldn't run on it for two weeks. Not fun, but I didn't care. I had finally achieved my goal of throwing the ball down! Do you know what I did when my leg healed? I went back out and tried to dunk again. I didn't care that I might get hurt because the joy I had in accomplishing something kept me going.

I hope that I will always have that attitude—to get back up and go back at it after I have been wounded. I see friends of mine model that around me—people who keep pursuing God and godly relationships after losing a spouse who betrayed them, people who say they'll give God another chance, people who don't let their parents' divorce define their view of God or love. They keep pursuing a life with a God who loves them and will heal their wounds.

This is what Jesus came for: to heal the wounds that have injured His people. That gives me hope.

Breaking the Cycle

○ Try to get to know yourself a little better this week.
Commit to spending ten minutes a day alone and in silence.
Consider this question: What makes me the way that I am?

○ Based on your thoughts, journal about your hopes, fears, and insecurities in an effort to identify some past experiences that have profoundly influenced who you are.

○ Take a chance to connect with other group members outside of your regular meeting time.

"GOD! YOU WALKED OFF AND LEFT US,
KICKED OUR DEFENSES TO BITS AND
STALKED OFF ANGRY.
COME BACK. OH PLEASE, COME BACK!
YOU SHOOK EARTH TO THE FOUNDATIONS,
RIPPED OPEN HUGE CREVASSES.
HEAL THE BREAKS!
EVERYTHING'S COMING APART AT THE SEAMS.
YOU MADE YOUR PEOPLE LOOK DOOM IN THE FACE,
THEN GAVE US CHEAP WINE TO DROWN OUR TROUBLES.
THEN YOU PLANTED A FLAG TO RALLY YOUR PEOPLE,
AN UNFURLED FLAG TO LOOK TO FOR COURAGE.
NOW DO SOMETHING QUICKLY, ANSWER RIGHT NOW,
SO THE ONE YOU LOVE BEST IS SAVED."

PSALM 60:1-5, THE MESSAGE

I hated that bee costume . . .

SESSION THREE
Falling Over

DO YOU REMEMBER WHAT LIFE WAS LIKE BEFORE IT HAD SHARP EDGES?

I can remember when life was innocent. I had a great experience growing up in South America. The area where we lived in Columbia was violent, but my parents shielded me from most of it. I always felt safe—maybe too safe. I remember jumping off high cliffs to impress girls (which, come to think of it, never really worked), and getting into all kinds of trouble thinking that I was Superman!

One time in particular, we were on a retreat with my parents' work team at a resort. While all the parents were having their meetings, the other kids and I had free rein. This place was pretty swanky, and it had its own zoo with shuttles to run you around. We were coming back from the zoo one day when I had an adventuresome—and disastrous—idea. I thought it would be cool to jump off the bus just before we stopped to show how tough I was. I think I had seen it in a movie, and once again, I was trying to impress some girl.

So . . . I stepped off the bus while it was going about ten miles an hour.

The doors of the bus were at the back with a step that went all the way to the pavement. I would be facing backwards when I stepped off the bus. By the time my feet hit the pavement, it was too late to catch my mistake. One second I was thinking, *Man, I am so cool,* and the next I was lying flat on the road. The momentum of my body, still moving at ten miles an hour, came to an immediate stop. While my head tomahawked into the blacktop I laid there, stunned, while my friends' laughter roared in the distance.

CAUSE AND EFFECT

Sometimes we feel so safe, so sheltered, so comfortable that we think our lives and ideals are invincible. Then reality steps in to remind us of our own vulnerability. Fortunately for me, I don't hold onto an unhealthy fear of asphalt today. A lot of us aren't so lucky. That initial experience of pain can result in a lifetime of self-protection, insecurity, and even addiction if left unchecked.

We all receive wounds in life. We fall over when we least expect it. We get embarrassed when we're trying to be brave. We get hurt when we think we're safe. In the last session, we looked at different kinds of wounds and the importance of identifying them. What happens when we don't identify our wounds? What happens when we don't process how we were hurt and why a seemingly safe situation wasn't so safe after all? How does that affect us, and how does it make us jaded?

I heard noted counselor and professor Dan Allender say that when we are wounded, we hide and blame. I see that happening in life. When we are flattened by something, it feels better to hold someone else responsible for our misery. We use sarcasm. We become bitter. We get mad. We guard our hearts in the wrong way by retreating instead of engaging. We become jaded and cynical.

When you've taken an embarrassing fall in life, what does retreating usually look like for you?

In what ways would you say you are cynical or jaded?

I believe that most of us are jaded in some way. Maybe we don't want to be, but because we've been hurt or disillusioned, we've hardened ourselves as a coping mechanism. It's often an unconscious act designed to protect what is left of our hearts.

For more information about the continuing teaching and counseling ministry of Dan Allender, visit *thepathlesschosen.com*.

Take a moment to do some self-discovery: In what ways has life not turned out the way you wanted it to?

How have you responded to that reality?

IT'S GOTTA BE SOMEBODY'S FAULT!

We start blaming when we stop believing the best in other people. We start doubting that people, and even God, are who they claim to be. Maybe you've experienced this disbelief. Maybe you've become someone who looks at everything with a critical eye.

I've been there. I used to tell people in a cheerful fashion that cynicism worked for me. It seemed like a more mature way of thinking. I mean, who really wants to be an idealist when you can be a cynic? As a cynic, you can act like everyone else is an idiot. I got really good at consistently looking at the negative aspect of every situation. I even prided myself on being able to see whatever "spin" others put on their viewpoint, but I was just another guy with a wound. Cynicism was my form of self-protection.

The problem with being cynical about one aspect of your life is that cynicism leaks into all aspects of life. The cynic will eventually become jaded to the core. Everything will be seen in a negative light until hope becomes something you used to believe in.

I know this all too well from experience. Life didn't turn out like I thought it would in my first ministry job. I thought I was in the perfect place to become powerful and popular. All my dreams for myself were going to come true. Only when they didn't, and I kept being passed over in favor of others, my heart became hard.

For an interesting movie about a recovering cynic and what brought hope back to his life, check out *Finding Forrester*.

What had been so pure for me earlier became a place of pain. As much as I wanted it to be, the problem wasn't the situation or the people involved—it was me. The reason I became bitter was that my pride was wounded. Things weren't turning out the way I had planned, and my heart was turning inward.

As a result, I lost the close relationships I had with coworkers, and I lost my heart for the work. As jadedness spread to all parts of my life, I began to distrust God's plan for me. I began to ask critical questions of everyone, including my family and my friends. I began to think the worst instead of the best.

Eventually, the end result came—I lost hope and went into despair. It seemed like life would never become better. I started believing the lie that this cynical, dark mood I lived in was all I could expect. Maybe you know that feeling. In fact, if you haven't been there at all, you'll probably get there someday. But—and here is where it gets good—there is hope.

WHAT? IT'S NOT ABOUT ME?

A lot of cynicism is rooted in the fact that we've been hurt and our dreams have not been fulfilled. Here is the deal, though: We are most often disappointed because most of our dreams are all about us. But—get ready for this—*this life isn't all about us.*

Take that in for a minute. It can be a hard realization.

When I make life all about me, I become sidetracked in trying to please myself or please others (which will win their approval, which will then please me). Cynicism brings us into the trap of selfishness. We start protecting our own stake in things—trying to control whatever situation we're in—so that others can't find the happiness we think we've been denied. It's not unlike when we were little kids who didn't want to share our toys. We become territorial and emotional.

> Take a realistic look at your life. Who is at the center of it? How can you tell?

Listen to "Starting Over" by Audio Adrenline from the *Jaded* playlist. Have you ever wanted a "do-over" with part of your life?

How have you blocked others from happiness (or even resented their happiness) because you were unhappy?

Being selfish keeps us from doing the right thing even when we clearly know what that right thing is. We may even *want* to do the right thing, but our selfishness stands in the way like a brick wall. My family took a vacation to the Caribbean over Christmas a couple of years ago. My sister and my brother had both gotten married, and their new spouses would be with them. In a short period of time, our family had changed significantly.

I was so excited for them both, but it was strange to be the only member of my family who was single. The crisis hit when my sister, Ginny, and her husband, Jorge, met up with us three days into the trip. They had been on their honeymoon but were joining us at Christmas dinner with plans to stay for the following week. The problem? The hotel where we were staying was sold out, and the newlyweds didn't have a room. The next problem? Everyone thought the best option was for me to give up my room and stay with my parents. Everyone, that is, except me.

I had specifically chosen to have my own king-sized bed and my own cabin because I felt out of place and a little weird about being the only one in my family without a significant other. (I admit it was a pride thing thrown in with some self-protection.) On the one hand, giving up my room and staying with my parents made sense, but on the other, it was incredibly painful. It brought up all the emotional garbage of being in my late twenties, single, and feeling like life was passing me by. I was happy for my siblings, but I was still selfish enough to want to hold onto the bit of independence and happiness that I could control.

I did it. I gave up my room and stayed nice and calm on the surface. But then I threw a private temper tantrum at God. I was seething on the inside. I didn't want to be selfless. I was bitter about my lot in life. My dreams were not coming true, and it hurt. My younger siblings were finding success in love and in life, and I seemed to be in a holding pattern. I hated being treated like a kid because I was the single person.

What I realized there in the middle of my angry, emotional tantrum was that I needed to die to myself. I needed to trust God. It was OK that I felt angry and frustrated, but I didn't have to dwell in that mind-set of resentment. A big part of moving on was remembering that life is about something bigger than just me.

Describe a time when giving up something important to you was difficult, even though you knew it was right.

What are some ways you try to insulate yourself from uncomfortable situations?

Why do you think it's so hard to let go of what we really want?

SO WHO'S IT ABOUT THEN?

OK, so if it isn't about us, is it about God? What does He have to say about it anyway? If we keep looking at the saga of the Israelites, we can find some relevant truths. In 586 B.C., King Nebuchadnezzar of Babylon destroyed Jerusalem and marched the remaining Jews out of the city, exiling them throughout his empire.

Although the world seemed like it had ended for God's people, they had not been forgotten. God raised up national champions like Esther, a young Jewish girl who actually became Queen of Persia and was able to speak up for the preservation of her people.

God also used the prophets who were in exile, such as Ezekiel, to encourage the Jews and to call them back to their faith. Ezekiel's prophecy is fascinating. God spoke very specifically to and through the prophet about His plan for the Jews.

> Read Ezekiel 36:21-24.
> Jot down any questions you have about this passage on the first read.

Most of the people of Israel probably didn't have access to a personal copy of the prophecy but could have heard this read to them. How do you think the people of Israel felt when they heard these words?

Ezekiel, whose name means "God strengthens," was born into a family of priests. Therefore, he combined the offices of both prophet and priest. As a member of the Zadok family, Ezekiel was among the aristrocracy taken into captivity by Nebuchanezzar of Babylon.

These people were mocked because of their faith in God. Describe a time you or someone you know was persecuted or put down for faith-related reasons. How did you or your friend respond?

God told His people that He had a plan for them. He was going to bring them back from captivity. Can you imagine what it felt like for those who had been in years of captivity to be told they would be released? Many of the younger people had actually been born during the exile—they had never even seen their homeland. Going home was a reality for which they had little frame of reference. Up to this point, many of them may have felt that there was no end in sight.

God said He had concern for His holy name. Why do you think that is important?

In what ways do we not take care of the holy name of God?

The most important thing in the universe to God is God. To learn more about this uncomfortable truth and how to live a God-centered life, pick up a copy of John Piper's book *Desiring God*.

God's heart was moved by the condition of His people. They were profaned (which means they were made fun of, cursed, and mocked) in their countries of exile. God took their hurt personally and decided to intervene. But there was a catch—it was not for their happiness or ease of mind that this would happen. It was because God Himself was being made to look bad.

God said He would take care of the Israelites because His reputation was at stake. Apparently these people who had once been pursuing other gods had made a change in their lives. In captivity, they were not known for worshiping other gods but only the one true God. God's people had returned to Him, and God began to act.

GOD'S HOLY NAME

God's name is a big deal to Him. In Exodus, when the Lord revealed His name to Moses, the tone with which He declared His name carried an air of majesty about it. The Hebrew people had a reverence when they mentioned the personal name of God. It was not something to be taken lightly. They did not use it commonly because they knew that it had power and deserved reverence. To use God's name lightly was to do so at their own risk.

Each time a scribe wrote God's name in the process of duplicating a manuscript, he would stand up, break his pen, and then go outside and bury the pen. The thought was that the name he wrote was so holy he shouldn't use that pen any longer.

> **In Scripture, people refer to God in different ways: The Lord Your God, God the Provider, Savior, and others. What are some of the names you use for God? Why are those designations meaningful to you?**

If you are a little confused about the name of God, let me clarify something. You may have seen a poster at some time that had fifty names of God and are now wondering, *What do you mean by the name of God?* You also may have been taught that the name of God is *Jehovah* or *Yahweh*. It can be confusing. Here are a couple of key ideas to consider:

1. There is a difference between the personal name of God and what we call *epithets*. Epithets are descriptive names that people gave to God out of their own experience of Him. *Jehovah Jireh* means "God the provider," but that is not God's actual name. A common word for God was *Adonai,* which basically means "lord or master." It is generic in its original meaning.

2. We do know how to spell God's name, but not how to pronounce it. His personal name is what scholars call the *tetragrammaton,* a word of four letters. In the Bible, it is usually translated as LORD in all capital letters. The word as it is spelled in Scripture, though, is YHVH. Written Hebrew is all consonants, so there would have been many different ways to pronounce this word depending on how you plugged in the vowels. Scribes would write the word *Adonai* beneath the name for God so people could replace God's name with *Adonai* when they were reading aloud. Because of that, the vowels from Adonai have been placed into the four consonants of God's name. Eventually, people started using those vowels to pronounce YHVH as Jehovah or Yahweh, but those are only substitutes. In fact, *Jehovah* was actually a German version. The soft Y in the name was converted to a J.

> "I will act for My own sake, indeed, My own, for how can I be defiled? I will not give My glory to another" (Isaiah 48:11).

Throughout the centuries, the name of God has been treated with care because God is serious about His name and His reputation. He is on a mission to make sure that all over the world, people know His name—that is, they understand who the true God of the universe is.

> Take a second and brainstorm some ways you can spread the reputation of God.

> If you can't see the ways God is at work around you, start praying that He will show it to you, as well as show you how you can take part in that work.

REVEALED THROUGH HIS PEOPLE

God is on a mission to reveal Himself to the world, making His name great. The primary tool He has used, is using, and will continue to use to accomplish this goal is us—His people:

"'I will honor the holiness of My great name, which has been profaned among the nations—the name you have profaned among them. The nations will know that I am Yahweh'—the declaration of the Lord GOD—'when I demonstrate My holiness through you in their sight'" (Ezekiel 36:23).

God's plan for being known is us. And that is humbling. God's plan for reconciling a lost and broken world to Himself is people—and that includes you and I right now. God will use our lives as a picture to show Himself to the world.

But often God does not choose to reveal Himself through a jaded person. Someone who is hardened and cynical does not reflect God's character well. God wants us to move past cynicism so we can provide hope. He has chosen to engage with you and me so that He can be shown as great, good, compassionate, and gracious through our lives.

> **What do you think when you hear that being cynical means your heart has hardened? Do you resonate with it? Get defensive? Other responses?**

> **Jot down some specific ways you can step away from the jaded cycle.**

God launched His plan to reveal Himself to the world through His people in Genesis 12:1-3. He promised that Abraham and his descendants would eventually be a blessing to all the peoples on earth. This would occur as God blessed His people with the knowledge of Himself. They, in turn, were to act as conduits through which that blessing would flow.

When there's bitterness in your life, you have to make a choice. You can stay where you are, remain bitter, and eventually stop feeling anything at all, or you can choose to see your wound as an opportunity. Your circumstances are not without purpose. They may be the result of bad choices or the fallen nature of this world, but God will use them regardless. Through your wound, God can show Himself to be real both to you and to those around you. You have a golden opportunity to experience God and to be used by Him.

Part of choosing to see your wound as an opportunity is placing yourself into God's story. His story is still continuing around us and throughout the world. Sometimes we don't see it, but God is still working to reconcile people to Himself. To put ourselves back into His story, rather than our own little tale, is to become hope-givers.

A hope-giver is someone who not only has hope but also instills it in others; someone who has ideals but is also trusting in God.

MAKE THE CHOICE

Here are two suggestions for seeing your wound as opportunity:

1. Learn through your circumstances. Every time you go though a discouraging season, pay attention to what God may be teaching you. God speaks powerfully during those times. From your wound, you might now know, for example, that you are stronger than you thought, that you should be more compassionate, that you don't react well to pressure, or that you react angrily when you are frustrated.

> Outline any discouraging circumstances that you're facing. What could God accomplish in you through these circumstances?

To begin to take the focus off yourself, find an opportunity to influence your community. You can do this through your church or a local organization, but if you need help in locating a place to make a difference, look at *voa.org*, the Volunteers of America web site, and search for an opportunity near you.

2. Choose to give yourself away by ministering to others. My dad once told me that serving others is never boring. Figure out a way to serve someone else in order to take the focus off of yourself. Find a place at your church or in your community. For example, serve in a soup kitchen or homeless shelter once a month. Or simply reach out to someone who needs a friend and build a connection.

> Write down one thing you can start doing that will help you take your eyes off yourself and toward God.

Being jaded is like being stuck in a holding pattern. You really want to get out, but it takes time. Use this struggle as a time to focus on God. Your faith and your circumstances are in a battle. It's hard to believe in God's power to heal when you are struggling, but it is in that struggle that God is actually the strongest. Paul the apostle learned that lesson, but he learned it through difficulty and struggle. We can learn from his words in 2 Corinthians 12:9-10:

"But He said to me, 'My grace is sufficient for you, for power is perfected in weakness.' Therefore, I will most gladly boast all the more about my weaknesses, so that Christ's power may reside in me. So because of Christ, I am pleased in weaknesses, in insults, in catastrophes, in persecutions, and in pressures. For when I am weak, then I am strong."

When we are cynical and weak but choose to trust God anyway, He shows Himself to be strong in our lives. In our weakness, we acknowledge that we are incapable of fixing ourselves. That's when God really takes center stage. Suddenly, we have hope, but we have hope because God has given it to us. Our weakness has become the avenue by which God reveals Himself to others around us.

Breaking the Cycle

○ Do you like to play the blame game? Prayerfully reflect on who, if anyone, you tend to blame for your unmet expectations about life. Ask the Holy Spirit to help you begin to sort through the truth of your feelings.

○ As a reminder of the importance of committing yourself to glorifying God, memorize Isaiah 48:11: "I will act for My own sake, indeed, My own, for how can I be defiled? I will not give My glory to another."

○ You are not on this journey alone. Spend some time hanging out with your group and hearing more about their life stories.

"GOD, GOD . . . MY GOD! WHY DID YOU DUMP

ME MILES FROM NOWHERE?

DOUBLED UP WITH PAIN, I CALL TO GOD

ALL THE DAY LONG. NO ANSWER. NOTHING.

I KEEP AT IT ALL NIGHT, TOSSING AND TURNING.

AND YOU! ARE YOU INDIFFERENT, ABOVE IT ALL,

LEANING BACK ON THE CUSHIONS OF ISRAEL'S PRAISE?

WE KNOW YOU WERE THERE FOR OUR PARENTS:

THEY CRIED FOR YOUR HELP AND YOU GAVE IT;

THEY TRUSTED AND LIVED A GOOD LIFE.

AND HERE I AM, A NOTHING—AN EARTHWORM,

SOMETHING TO STEP ON, TO SQUASH.

EVERYONE POKES FUN AT ME;

THEY MAKE FACES AT ME, THEY SHAKE THEIR HEADS:

'LET'S SEE HOW GOD HANDLES THIS ONE;

SINCE GOD LIKES HIM SO MUCH, LET HIM HELP HIM!'"

PSALM 22:1-8, THE MESSAGE

Back in the saddle . . . .

SESSION FOUR

Rebirth

THERE IS SOMETHING SPECIAL ABOUT STARTING FRESH. Something just seems right about new beginnings. This is particularly apparent when it comes to babies.

This past winter I became an uncle for the first time. Maybe you have been an uncle or an aunt several times over so it isn't that big a deal, but for our family this was the first grandchild. It was the biggest event in the last twenty years. To make it even more exciting, my sister went into labor a week early, which threw us all for a loop as our carefully laid plans came screeching to a halt. My mom flew into town on an hour's notice to help, and I immediately morphed into her personal assistant. I rearranged my schedule to be the errand boy—not that I minded. It was better to do that than sit at the hospital waiting around.

When the baby finally arrived, it was amazing! She was the most beautiful little girl I had ever seen. She was so tiny, and it overwhelmed me that suddenly there was this completely new person I was related to. Her whole life was ahead of her, and there was so much potential yet to be tapped within her. As she struggled with the new lights and sounds, trying to figure out what was going on, I wanted to guard my niece against this harsh world so that she wouldn't feel the same pains that I had encountered.

It made me wonder what life would look like for me if I got to start over again. What would I do differently? What would you do differently if you had a chance to start life again? What unrealized potential still lies inside in you?

STARTING OVER

Life doesn't stay fresh forever, though. In the process of living, we get wounded, and we react. It's easy to become driven, bitter, aloof, or angry. We spend our lives trying to please people who are indifferent to us. We argue in our heads with people who don't give us a second thought. We fight our inner demons of self-doubt and self-loathing. We compete with people who are friends and sometimes drive them away.

When life turns dark, we feel like we are struggling underwater with the surface retreating quickly above us. What would we give to be free of this burden and to live life the way it could be lived, making the most of all our potential?

Everybody has some "could have been's" in their lives. Take Uncle Rico from *Napoleon Dynamite* for example. It's sadly funny that he lives in a van and videos himself throwing a football. He is constantly reliving the glory days or, in his case, the "almost-happened" glory days.

To a lesser extent (hopefully), we all think about what might have been in our lives. We all wish we could start over at some level. If only we could undo the past or do it just a little differently, we think we would be much happier. That's not to say that we aren't thankful for the wisdom and experience we've gained through the struggles and hard times, but if we could just do it over again with the wisdom we've gained, we would do it in a heartbeat. I can't tell you how many of my friends at some point have said, "Man, if I could go back to high school with what I know now, life would be so different." It's tragic that some of us are still trying to recapture something we missed out on or lost in our past.

If we could start over, we could get past our hurts, our disillusionment, our jadedness, our cynicism. Life would be fresh. It would be new. We would have a blank slate, at least emotionally, so that we wouldn't feel the pain of our past any longer.

Though we can't go back, I believe that there is an opportunity to be free, experience a new way of living, and move past a jaded existence. It's not as simple as just praying a prayer and everything being fixed in your life. That may happen for you out of God's kindness, but for most of us, like everything else worthwhile, it is a process.

Napoleon Dynamite is a great movie about seizing opportunities, no matter how small. Make an evening out of viewing it with your group of friends. Serve tater tots.

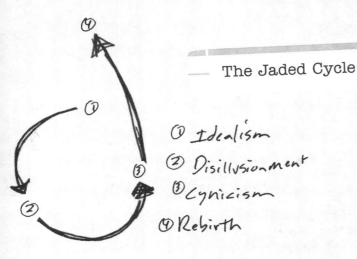

The Jaded Cycle

① Idealism
② Disillusionment
③ Cynicism
④ Rebirth

OK, so you are jaded. And with each passing disappointment, you are become more and more cynical. The good news is that through Christ, you can escape from the spiral into hope. The hope you can find is so fresh and new that it feels like being reborn. Not rebirth in the sense of receiving salvation through Christ, but bebirth in seeing life through hope instead of cynicism. That feels new and fresh. It is my prayer that you will find a new way to live that doesn't deny your pain; it moves through it.

Do you believe it is possible to be free from the past?

Is there any value in remembering the past? Why?

How do you think God wants you to relate to your past?

HOPE FOR GOD'S PEOPLE

Like most things, integrating this new way of hopeful living starts with God's plan. Let's pick up with the story of Israel. If you remember, because of their failure in following God, the Israelites were deported and exiled from their country by the Babylonians.

God got their attention when they lost the one thing they valued above all others—their homeland. They were stuck in a country far from home, experiencing persecution, and facing the threat of losing their cultural identity. I can't imagine a much more depressed group. Not only were they separated from all they knew as home, but they also felt like God had either abandoned them, hated them, or maybe didn't exist at all. In the midst of this pain and struggle, God spoke words of incredible hope to His people through the prophet Ezekiel.

Read Ezekiel 36:24-28.

In the middle of their pain, though, God began to do something new. In verse 24, He told the Israelites that they would have their heart's desire, the promise He had given to them years earlier—they would return to their homeland. Hearing that promise was life-changing. Hope must have begun to blossom into their hearts. The end to their waiting was near.

But first there were some things God had to do in their lives before He brought them back.

First, God would cleanse the people from their impurities and get rid of all the idols they had worshiped. Remember, God used Hosea's life to paint a picture of what the people of Israel were doing when they worshiped both God and false idols. Under God's direction, Hosea married a prostitute who was unfaithful to him, but Hosea went and found her and brought her back to himself.

We have talked about Gomer's perspective, but what about Hosea? I couldn't imagine going out to the street corner and buying my wife back from a pimp and bringing her home to live with me again, completely forgiven. Yet that is what Hosea did as a picture of what God was going to do for these exiled people. He would buy them back.

We are in the same position as the people of Israel were long ago. We also seek other gods and worship them, prostituting ourselves to whatever is convenient. Rather than choosing intimacy with God, we have sought

Jesus built on the idea of the new heart, telling the pharisee Nicodemus in John 3 that he needed to be "born again." This experience that Jeremiah, Ezekiel, and Jesus spoke about is so dramatic that it can only be described as starting over, or having a brand new life.

our joy in temporary things. Time and time again, we look to things that spoil and rot to give us lasting satisfaction. God says those are false gods—they can never satisfy us, and they only drive a wedge between us and our Maker. We must be cleansed by His power and His forgiveness.

What would it mean to you to fully accept God's cleansing?

God has said that He will forgive us from all unrighteousness if we just call on Him (1 John 1:9). If there is something that God is bringing to your mind that you need to confess right now, take a minute and ask for His healing in your life. Beyond the cleansing, God also made a spectacular promise—new hearts:

"I will give you a new heart and put a new spirit within you; I will remove your heart of stone and give you a heart of flesh" (Ezekiel 36:26).

This isn't a description of some weird pagan ritual. Rather, it was God's way of communicating to His people that He would give them a new way of thinking, one that focused on seeking God. He would change their very outlook on life.

Though God gives every Christ-follower a new heart when they choose to follow Jesus the first time, we often fail to live out that newness. Our choices cause pain, and that pain along with other wounds begin to build up scar tissue around our new hearts. The resulting "tough heart" may allow us to survive, but it doesn't let us truly live. From time to time, we need to be woken up to the fact that God has given us a heart of flesh. We need to be revived. We need to open ourselves up to the possibility of life again. Or at least that's how it was for me.

It was in the midst of my cynicism that I read this passage for the first time in years. I felt God speaking to me. In my bitterness, I had become hard-hearted and had withdrawn from any emotion toward God. I was cold as ice. Why? I had encountered the death of a dream. Life wasn't what I thought it was going to be. I felt that God had

The prophets Isaiah and Jeremiah, as well as Ezekiel, also lived during the exile. They interpreted the Israelite exile to Babylon as divine judgment. Yet they also saw God's redemptive plan through it. One result of the exile was that Israel gained a more profound appreciation for for the Law and Prophets, or what we know as the Old Testament. They also came to believe more strongly in the universal rule and sovereignty of God, a characteristic that would later keep them pure during the rise of the Greek culture.

abandoned me and maybe that this church thing wasn't all it was cracked up to be. Yet as I read, I found God calling me back to Himself. My heart began to thaw. He reawakened my passion for Him. Hope stirred in my soul.

What does Ezekiel 36:26 mean to you personally?

Do you believe that God can renew your spirit?

THE FREEDOM CHOICE

At the bottom of the jaded cycle there is a choice: move further into disillusionment or be filled with hope. The secret is in what I call the "freedom choice." I spent a long time trying to figure out how to describe this in words until I stumbled on it in Scripture. It was one of those "aha!" moments.

In Romans 5, Paul offers insight for the jaded. Verse 1 says,

"Therefore, since we have been declared righteous by faith, we have peace with God through our Lord Jesus Christ."

Amazing! The conflict between God and us has been healed through Jesus. Although we have injured God repeatedly, He has never given up on us. He continues to re-engage with us to the point that He gave His own Son, Jesus Christ, for us when He didn't owe us anything. Because of our rebellion, we were considered enemies of God. But through His sacrifice, Jesus ended the conflict in our relationship with God—He brought peace.

The key to all this is that we must make a decision about how we are going to react to the world we still live in. We must somehow choose to live in the consciousness of our new life. That means living in a constant state of trust in God regardless of our circumstances. Read to verse 3:

Paul wrote the book of Romans to a church struggling to know who they were in the world. To make matters worse, the Roman Emperor Nero was beginning to unleash a terrible wave of persecution. No wonder Paul used terms like *perservere* and *character* in Romans 5.

"And not only that, but we also rejoice in our afflictions, because we know that affliction produces endurance . . ."

Read this verse out loud. How would you describe the key to living in a state of trust in God regardless of your life circumstances?

Listen to "The Hope and the Healing—Part II." Your leader will send it to you via e-mail.

From my perspective, here's the point: Paul said we are to rejoice in our afflictions. Was he kidding? Had he lost his mind? None of us want to rejoice in our afflictions. To rejoice means more than just accepting the tough times and wounds of our lives. Paul wanted Jesus' followers to be excited about those difficulties. It doesn't seem to make sense, so he must have had a reason behind his words.

How do you feel when you are in the midst of difficulties?

Why do you think Paul would want us to rejoice in suffering?

As you read on, you see his reason. In verses 4 and 5, Paul described a progression that happens in us when we choose to rejoice:

". . . endurance produces proven character, and proven character produces hope. This hope does not disappoint, because God's love has been poured out in our hearts through the Holy Spirit who was given to us" (Romans 5:4-5).

The word *affliction* from Romans 5:3 comes from the root word *thlibo* meaning "to crush, press, compress, or squeeze." It's a fitting description, since circumstances can often feel as though they are too heavy to carry and are pressing in on us.

If you follow on with Paul, you see that he says affliction produces something. Out of affliction, endurance is birthed. The afflictions, or tough times, give us stamina in this life. They create some substance to our will. That endurance then produces proven character, which is a collection of the ideals and standards by which our lives are defined. We become people who have moral fiber through the endurance and afflictions that we go through.

Then proven character produces what the world is craving: hope. It's what our souls long for—hope that people can change, that we can change, that poverty can decrease, that childhood diseases will vanish, that racism will disappear, that war will end, that the kingdom of God will not only be a dream but a reality on this planet. Can you follow the chain of events?

What's your first response to the thought that affliction opens the door for hope?

Have you seen any evidence of this process in your own life?

In what circumstance do you need hope?

MY STORY

Here's how I've grappled with this in my own life. It's one thing to talk about being jaded in general and another to talk about how you have personally been jaded. There are several places in my life in which I have struggled with this, but the one that has been the hardest is the church.

Since my dad was a missionary in Colombia, I have been around church my entire life. I have had the rich heritage of a godly family. It wasn't until I was in my twenties that I became jaded about the church. I think it had something to do with how the business model had invaded the church. Now I am all for excellence, having good systems, working hard, and the clarity of thought that our friends in the corporate sector have helped us with in the church.

But something happens when you remove the heart of a church— accepting people who are far from God—and replace it with a growth model. Church becomes more about strategy than love, and people's value becomes linked to what they can contribute. I saw this too many times both in myself and in my friends, and I began to lose heart.

Then I removed myself from engaging the conflict and embracing my afflictions and became hard and distant, preferring the comfort of cynicism. My walk with God began to suffer because I checked out on Him and focused more on my perceived wounds, feeling sorry for myself every chance I got. I had seen too many of my friends falter in their walks with God and burn out on the machine the church had become. I began to feel that if this was church, I would rather not be a part of it. I began to contemplate leaving the ministry and pursuing a medical degree (at least the money would be much better).

Then God began to speak to me again. Through Ezekiel 36, He gave me a dream and a hope. I was reading my Bible one day when a sense of God's presence cascaded over me, and I realized that He still had plans for me, plans that I had to pursue regardless of the hardship. It meant leaving my church, my friends, and my comfort to start a journey to rediscovering God and what it meant for me to follow Him. I decided to reject cynicism and chose to follow hope. And it has made all the difference.

What will it take for you to hope and dream again?

"Dear friends, when the fiery ordeal arises among you to test you, don't be surprised by it, as if something unusual were happening to you. Instead, as you share in the sufferings of the Messiah rejoice, so that you may also rejoice with great joy at the revelation of His glory" (1 Peter 4:12-13).

What dream do you believe God has placed in your life that you are scared to name or share with others?

WHAT WILL YOU DO?

We must reject cynicism completely because it robs us of hope. It doesn't work for us. It only makes us run and hide from life instead of embracing and rejoicing during the trials that come our way. It pushes us to distrust God, to call Him *out* instead of calling *on* Him.

The fact is that God uses many trials to put us in the right place emotionally as well as geographically to move into the next phase of our spiritual lives. The pain still hurts, but with that knowledge in mind, we can walk through it with a sense of hope rather than jadedness. If we are only on a happiness quest, we will never make it through the tough times, but if we are on a hope quest, we can go through anything. God has made peace with us and will give us hope if we embrace Him.

Here are a few practical ways to step away from cynicism:

- **CHOOSE TO LET GOD GIVE YOU A NEW HEART.** This is the most important thing. You can't change your heart on your own. You need to ask God to work in your life and give you a heart of flesh instead of a heart of stone. Ask God for healing and regeneration.

- **CHOOSE TO BELIEVE THE BEST ABOUT OTHERS INSTEAD OF THE WORST.** This is not easy. You will have to discipline yourself not to fall back into the same old patterns. Others will drag you down, and it will be very hard to stay out of conversations with other people who are still cynical. In a similar theme, watch what you talk about with your friends. Have you noticed that you tend to talk about certain things with certain friends? With some of your friends, you talk about people of the opposite sex, with some you gossip, with some you talk sports or fashion, but you typically stay on the same themes. If you are cynical, I bet you have friends with whom you talk about the same cynical themes. You need to either change themes or change friends.

- **SPEND TIME IN GOD'S WORD.** If you need a place to start, try Psalm 18. Worshiping God brings hope. Just spend some time every day reading and thinking about it, and you will be amazed at how God's peace will seep into your life.

Which one of these changes will you make first? I suggest you pick one and begin tonight. Pick another tomorrow and another for the next day. Put a number next to them now: 1, 2, 3. The results may be gradual, but they will be longer-lasting if you grow into them.

Fighting your way back from a jaded place may take a long time. It is not an easy process to break the cycle. Bitterness can be addictive, but hope prevails. If we choose to engage with God the same way He has connected with us, we will find a life that is far different than we can imagine. It will be a firm life, like a tree with deep roots. And when the storms of circumstances threaten us, we will stand tall.

Breaking the Cycle

○ Read Romans 8. Write down all the things Paul says in that passage about who you are. Keep that list on a mirror to remind yourself this week that you have a new heart.

○ When you have conversations this week, make an effort to compliment the person you are talking to. Pick out something good about them and let them know about it. It will encourage them and also put you in a mode of thinking the best about others.

○ Don't forget about your group. E-mail some of your group with specific things you appreciate about who they are.

"LONG ENOUGH, GOD—YOU'VE IGNORED ME LONG ENOUGH.

I'VE LOOKED AT THE BACK OF YOUR HEAD LONG ENOUGH.

LONG ENOUGH I'VE CARRIED THIS TON OF TROUBLE,

LIVED WITH A STOMACH FULL OF PAIN.

LONG ENOUGH MY ARROGANT ENEMIES

HAVE LOOKED DOWN THEIR NOSES AT ME.

TAKE A GOOD LOOK AT ME, GOD, MY GOD;

I WANT TO LOOK LIFE IN THE EYE,

SO NO ENEMY CAN GET THE BEST OF ME

OR LAUGH WHEN I FALL ON MY FACE.

I'VE THROWN MYSELF HEADLONG INTO YOUR ARMS—

I'M CELEBRATING YOUR RESCUE.

I'M SINGING AT THE TOP OF MY LUNGS,

I'M SO FULL OF ANSWERED PRAYERS."

PSALM 13, THE MESSAGE

Tis better to serve than to be . . .

SESSION FIVE
Hope and Healing

MY NOSE IS SERIOUSLY MESSED UP.

I was in sixth grade when a neighborhood kid kicked me in the face with a soccer ball during a pick-up game. All I remember was a sharp blow and something not feeling quite right. From then until I was 27, I had a tough time breathing through my nose. I thought it was just allergies, but one day I decided to have it checked out.

I asked around and found a great ear, nose, and throat doctor who agreed to see me. The doctor inserted a piece of metal that looked like a car antenna into my nostril. Since I've never been impaled on anything before, this was a new and uncomfortable experience.

The antenna was actually a camera. When the doctor finished taking a tour of the inside of my face, he spoke in a tone of hushed awe. He told me he had never seen anything that looked so normal on the outside be so messed up on the inside—somehow that was both comforting and distressing at the same time. At least I knew I wasn't crazy for having trouble breathing, but what did he mean by that technical term "messed up"?

The good doctor told me that they were going to perform a septoplasty, which means that they would completely rearrange the bones inside my nose. They also were going to do some work in my sinuses to make them wider. With that decided, we set a date for the surgery.

It was mildly horrific. I mean, I'm not trying to be a baby, but I hate being put under anesthesia—and the recovery was no fun at all. When I woke up after surgery, I was so thirsty, an ocean of icy water would not have been enough; and the next couple of days, I felt like there was something large and painful up my nose. Finally, after a full week of doing nothing around the house but waiting for my body to heal, the doctor removed all the things he had put in my face to provide support and help me recover. I was finally free.

Listen to "All Will Be Well" by The Gabe Dixon Band from your *Jaded* playlist.

Can you give yourself permission to believe it's true?

RECOVERY

It was weird to be finished with all the procedures, recovery, pain, and discomfort. Now what? Having jumped through all the hoops, what was next? The answer was simply to live and enjoy the healing and new nose that I had received. It was awesome to be able to get enough oxygen whenever I needed it. I didn't realize how bad things had been until I was healed. I slept better at night just because I could breathe normally. I could play sports better because of the change. All I had to do was enjoy my new state of being.

Here's why I share my nose story. Hopefully, at some time or another, we all end up at the same place I did after recovery. When you are finally healed, you start wondering, *What's next?* What do I do with my life now?

Our wounds mark our lives. Dealing with them occupies our time. They focus our energies. They give us something to blame or hold onto for motivation or strength. Even if we're angry about our situation, that rage gives us strength. It makes us feel good about our point of view even as it erodes our soul. Once the anger or the hurt or the injury is healed, what do we do with all of the time and energy we put into it?

To complicate things, many of us fear success more than failure anyway. What will happen when we are healed? What will we do then? This is a major obstacle for many young adults. We have become so comfortable in our cynical, broken lives that we wouldn't trade them for health because we wouldn't know what to do with it.

Have you ever felt the fear of success? What potential success are you afraid of?

What success would cause such a huge change in your life that it would be daunting?

Often we begin to have success in being well, but then it becomes too hard to maintain that success. We would rather sabotage ourselves so that we have an excuse for why we don't do more. Why do you think we do that?

What do you think God's attitude is concerning people who hide from success?

I want you to know a secret that very few followers of Jesus realize. Some people acknowledge its truth, but not many people let this secret sink in and impact the way they live their lives. The secret is this: The story of God and His people is still ongoing today. It's not simply an ancient story bound into a set of Scriptures—it's not over! It's a story that is happening now, one that we get to enter into if we allow ourselves to be healed from our wounds and cynicism. Further, this story is an adventure. God is still here, desperately trying to enter into relationship with the people who have chosen to follow other gods instead of Him.

Do you believe that God is still involved in this world?

Author and speaker Steven James offers a great perspective on the continuing biblical narrative in his book *Story: Recapture the Mystery*. Reading it will offer a creative aspect to your understanding of the redemptive story that God has been writing throughout all time.

What have you seen as evidence that He is still involved here on earth?

Deism is defined as the belief, based solely on reason, in a God who created the universe and then abandoned it, assuming no control over life, exerting no influence on natural phenomena, and giving no supernatural revelation.

Some people believe that God has removed Himself from the world and that He merely controls it from a distance or through things He set in motion a long time ago, such as gravity or the law of entropy. In that view the world is like an elaborate mechanism that God created. However, the Bible never portrays God like that. The God you see throughout the Bible is intimately concerned and connected to this world. He knows us by name and sees everything. He talks to people. He hears their prayers, and when He chooses to, He changes reality through the miraculous.

When we are jaded, we quit believing because we doubt everything. We question the truth of God's compassion, love, and care because of our personal pain. We take our wounded heart off the table, and we hide. Being jaded keeps us from believing that God has a purpose and plan for all of creation. Our disbelief makes us forget that this life is not just about waiting for Jesus to return or for us to die and go to heaven. God wants us to do something with the seventy or so years that He has given us on this planet.

In what ways do you find yourself doubting?

What do you think God wants us to do with our time here on earth? What about you, specifically?

NO MORE HAPPINESS QUEST

When we become jaded, we can't see beyond the fact that we are unhappy. Because of our disillusionment, we often tune out God when He alone can heal us. God has a plan, and when He renews our heart and sense of healthy optimism, He doesn't just do it so we can stuff ourselves with pretty things; He has something in mind for us. He has a mission, a new quest that far surpasses our personal happiness quest.

Do you want your life to matter—to be about something great, something lasting? I do. I want that more than anything. I want to be someone who made a difference in my time here. I believe God does this through the one thing that is opposite of cynicism and jadedness—hope. God wants us to have hope.

Hope starts by believing that God desires good things for us. But many of us don't trust that God has our best interests in mind. Jeremiah, a prophet who lived during the same time as Ezekiel and Hosea, talked to the people of Israel (and to us) about this when they were still in captivity. Read these verses out loud:

"'For I know the plans I have for you'—[this is] the LORD's declaration—'plans for [your] welfare, not for disaster, to give you a future and a hope. You will call to Me and come and pray to Me, and I will listen to you. You will seek Me and find Me when you search for Me with all your heart'" (Jeremiah 29:11-13).

It's amazing to hear God say He has plans for His people. He not only remembers them but has something specific in mind for them. I think it's awesome that He doesn't make His statement in generalities. He doesn't just have some random, casually thought-out plans—He has plans for our welfare, not disaster, for a future and a hope. He said this isn't any normal plan, but plans for a great future.

It's hard to see that truth sometimes when the hurt is so heavy in our present circumstances. The key is to remember God is not finished with us and has a working plan in which we are currently involved. Plus, God is moving right now—not just in the future. God has extended the invitation to partner with Him to bring about His kingdom fully on the earth as it is in heaven.

> **What kinds of things might keep you from believing that God is at work in the world right now?**

Jeremiah was born in the village of Anathoth, north of Jerusalem, as the son of a priest. His ministry spanned more than forty years, and throughout it, he supported social and religious reform. He never had a family of his own. His singleness was meant to be an illustration of the barrenness of a land under judgment.

What kinds of things might keep you from believing that God is at work in your life right now?

The Bible shows that God is actively moving behind the scenes. In what ways do you see Him moving in your life or in the lives of people around you?

"I will place My law within them and write it on their hearts. I will be their God, and they will be My people" (Jeremiah 31:33).

Also God gave the exiles a specific promise. Not only did He have a great plan, but He also revealed their role in it. He told them their destiny in verses 12-13:

"You will call to Me and come and pray to Me, and I will listen to you. You will seek Me and find Me when you search for Me with all your heart."

What are the first two or three things that come to your mind when you read those verses?

In your own words, what did God mean by this promise?

God told the people that they would return to Him. He would get their hearts back. God will get your heart back too when you focus your quest on Him. He has promised that He will respond.

YOUR NEW QUEST

Now here is the big idea that you need to wrap your mind around—God wants us to be people who exchange our happiness quest for something that really brings us joy. He wants us to start a hope quest.

That means we need to be people who live this life in such a way that we seek after God—with all our hearts. This quest will make you someone whose life is defined by hope—hope for the future and hope that God will do something great in your lifetime.

I don't think that means that you have to be the kind of optimist who annoys the people around with your constantly cheerful mood; that's not what hope really is. Think about it: Hope, by its very definition, means that things in your life are imperfect. To have hope is to recognize the pain and disappointment of your current situation. After all, if everything is great as it currently is, then what do you really need to hope for? No, hope is not just screwing on a smile and acting like everything is OK. Hope is, however, making the choice to believe in something bigger than your circumstances.

To choose hope is to choose to believe that God is not absent but present; that He is not apathetic but compassionate; and that He is not lazy but at work in your life, regardless of what the circumstances might suggest. But choosing hope is more than just acknowledging its presence. Choosing hope requires action. The action you choose to take will further help your life be defined by hope rather than disappointment.

What does it mean to you to be defined by hope?

How can you give up your happiness quest to be someone who seeks hope?

How do we let our lives be defined by hope? I believe it is by being "hope-givers," people who inspire others to hope that God is out there and has a plan for them too.

People are the primary tools God has decided to use to show hope to those who need to believe it's real. Hope is in a much smaller supply than despair in our world. But we can choose to become more than just someone's friend; we can make hope tangible and alive all around us.

Tom Rath wrote about this concept in his book *Vital Friends*. He studied the effect friends have on our lives, then laid out statistics and anecdotes about people who became homeless when they had no significant relationships in their lives. He said the question that needs to be answered by everyone is "Who expects me to be somebody?"

I believe we all need someone who expects the best out of us, someone who invests in our lives and cares with more than just words. I have a friend, Brad, who modeled this. Brad became connected with a guy named Paul who had just been sent to prison for selling drugs at a concert. They met by phone a week before the concert because Paul's brother, who was concerned about Paul but living in Africa at the time, asked Brad to make the connection. Brad believed the best in Paul and decided to invest in his life even though Paul didn't have anything to offer in return.

For six months, they corresponded through mail, and Brad began to mail Paul a Bible study called *Experiencing God*. He couldn't send it directly because the prison wouldn't accept a large book, so Brad painstakingly cut each page of each lesson out of the workbook and mailed it piecemeal to his friend. A couple of months into this discussion, Paul gave his heart to the Lord in his prison cell.

Things haven't gone perfectly since Paul got out of jail, but over the past three years, he has become a far different person because of Brad's investment. He now has a steady job and is following a call to ministry. When you ask him what made the difference, his immediate answer is, "Brad invested in me."

The point is that the wounded are all around us—people who are jaded and cynical. You can choose to actively live out a picture of the characteristics of the kingdom of God. And in doing that, you will not only be helping them; you will be moving closer and closer to your own life being defined by those same characteristics.

Who do you need to show hope to? If God is putting someone on your mind right now, write their name below.

What will you do to invest your life into them?

By the way, here's something else to keep in mind: If you can't be that person's friend in a way that doesn't feel forced, you should probably hold off. There's a fine line between investing in someone for the right reasons and doing it to win points or make ourselves feel good. No one wants to be our "project." You must be willing to make the investment without knowing what the outcome will be.

WEIGHING THE RISK
Some of us wonder if we can trust this hope-giving thing. Can we trust that God will go all the way with us? Will we be putting ourselves out there one more time only to start the cycle all over again? How can you trust what God says?

Last session, we studied a progression of character-building events found in Romans 5:1-5. It went like this:

Affliction ──→ Endurance ──→ Character ──→ Hope

Now check out the verses that come directly after Paul described that progression:

"For while we were still helpless, at the appointed moment, Christ died for the ungodly. For rarely will someone die for a just person—though for a good person perhaps someone might even dare to die. But God proves His own love for us in that while we were still sinners Christ died for us!" (Romans: 5:6-8).

Even before we knew God, Jesus gave His life for us—all of us who are sick, wounded, and needy. He gave His life for us even though by our actions, we had proven ourselves to be His enemies.

We often read this passage so quickly that we miss a huge aspect. The first word of the passage is *for*. This word matters because it is a connector. We often go right past it because we want to think about the timing of God's dying for the ungodly and how great it was that He cared so much. But the nature of the word *for* connects it to the verse just above. So go back and read Romans 5:3-5 again:

"And not only that, but we also rejoice in our afflictions, because we know that affliction produces endurance, endurance produces proven character, and proven character produces hope. This hope does not disappoint, because God's love has been poured out in our hearts through the Holy Spirit who was given to us."

Do you see it in a different light? Paul wrote that because of God's love for us, we can trust that we have a hope that does not disappoint. But he didn't leave it there. I think he threw down this proof for God's love in verses 6-8. There was no little subtitle between verses 5 and 6 in Paul's original letter. These were connected thoughts. Paul was telling us that we can trust the hope that comes from God because Jesus proved that God can be trusted by His sacrifice on the cross. That sacrifice came at the perfect time—when we needed it most.

Jesus came to earth to give us hope, and He proved it through the life He gave up. The Scripture says that He did it at the right time, the appointed moment, the specific time that He had designated to die—not one second earlier or later. Sounds like a tight timetable. That means we can trust that God already has gone to desperate lengths to make sure His plan will work. We can trust His timing. We can have hope because of the work He has done and continues to do.

What do you think about the fact that Jesus went the distancefor you?

The word for "appointed moment" in Romans 5:6 is *kairos*. The word indicates more than simply a chronological succession of moments. Instead, it is a specific, thought-out, unique point in time—the perfect moment for the event to occur. It's a moment that's full of possibility.

In what practical ways can you trust God with His plan for your life?

What areas are you still holding back from trusting God?

Listen to "The Hope and the Healing—Part III." Your group leader will send it to you via e-mail.

BE AN AGENT OF CHANGE

You can literally change the life of another person through hope. All it takes to become that kind of person are the choices to live in a certain way:

- Be someone who gives hope to others.
- Be someone who will put others before yourself.
- Be a giver, not a taker.
- Be someone who is defined by the hope quest.

God uses all kinds of people to do His work. He can even turn things that were broken or evil into forces for good. It's amazing to consider that the people God consistently used throughout the Bible were not perfect. They were not emotionally stable or even particularly righteous. They were regular—broken and regular.

Dr. Steve is a psychiatrist and a friend of mine. We were chatting about this the other day. He thinks it's funny that God used some people in the Bible who he would have diagnosed with some sort of mental illness. Dr. Steve says that David (his mood swings), Peter (how dramatic he was, even jumped out of a boat to walk on water), Hosea (married a prostitute), Elijah (called down fire from heaven and then hid in a cave) all had troubling symptoms.

Yet they were the ones God used to change the world. He's still using people with troubles today, and that's good news for another wounded, regular guy like me.

MAKE PROACTIVE DECISIONS

It's great to have a life that is about living and not about criticizing. However, you can slip back into a jaded mind-set if you don't get into new habits as a hope-giver. Start working right now. One of the best proactive decisions you can make is to form relationships with people who are further along in their journey with Christ than you are. Who are the people who challenge you to be a person of hope? This may mean that you have to redefine your best friends. Ask yourself: Who inspires me to be my best? Then get close to that person. Set up lunch or coffee with them.

Can you think of someone who would be a positive role model in your life? Who is it? Which qualities in his or her life do you admire?

You must also decide to look for hope. Looking for hope is like looking for the seasons to change. It's like looking for trees blooming in the spring. Just start looking around you for people who are starting to change. If they show interest in spiritual things, start a friendship with them. If someone is changing, celebrate with them.

Where do you see hope around you right now?

How can you come alongside that person or situation you see hope already moving in?

REGAIN YOUR IDEALISM

What? I spent an entire chapter talking about how idealism and pride are linked and how we need to run from it—and now we need it back?

Yes, but this is a different. What we need to regain is *mature* idealism—the ability to dream in an unselfish way, to dream about how things could and should be if we gave ourselves away unselfishly. We are not dreaming about what we can have, but what we can give. In my life it means risking it all by starting a church and watching God move through that community to make it a place where people are hope-givers.

Dreaming is all about passion. Can passion be reawakened in your life? I firmly believe that God is calling us to dream great dreams about how we can provide hope to the world. This is a new call to a new kind of idealism. It's not one of pride or one that demands the world accommodate our selfish demands.

Instead, it's a call that believes the best of what can be, one that brings hope to others and to the world. It's a call to participate in bringing about the kingdom of God. It's a call to serve amongst the poor and needy. It's a call to carry the gospel to the end of the earth. It's a call to start serving in our churches instead of criticizing them. Through all these actions, we display that we are dominated by hope grounded in the plans and purposes of God. This world needs idealism that awakens the passion that lies deep within people and calls them to tap into unused reservoirs of goodness and to do great deeds for God.

What awakens passion in your life?

What dream is out there that you feel God is calling you to but you are scared to tell people?

What would it take for you to start the path to realizing that dream?

I saw this passion in my parents when they left their comfortable homes in the United States to move to Bogotá, Colombia, in the mid-seventies. They felt that God was calling them to leave everything they knew to make a difference in people's lives.

The problem was that although Colombia was a wonderful country, it was also troubled and violent, and we lived there during the height of the violence. I remember having to take different routes to school in the mornings to avoid being kidnapped. Many nights there were gunfights on the street outside our home. During the worst of the conflict, we would wake up during the night to the lights and sounds of bombs going off in the city as drug lords flexed their muscles to influence elections.

Things were bad enough that when we thought we heard thunder, we assumed that it was a bombing instead. There were days we couldn't leave our homes because of the high security risk concerning Americans. The U.S. embassy strongly urged missionaries and Americans living overseas to return to the States, and there was a mass exodus of missionaries who returned to safety.

My parents and a few others felt differently about the situation. I remember my mom saying that God wanted us to stay, and we were going to trust in His protection. Now that sounds kind of crazy and idealistic, but I think they felt God was asking them to trust Him regardless of the circumstances.

In time, we could see a reward for their courage. God responded with the most fruitful ministry season of their experience in Colombia. God awakened a spiritual hunger in people that had not been there before. The people also saw that they could trust the missionaries who stayed behind because they didn't leave when the times got difficult.

If you ask them if it was worth it to trust God and to dream, they will tell you undeniably "yes." They were able to share the story of Jesus with literally thousands of people, and it would not have been possible if they had not chosen to dream the impossible and commit their lives fully.

As you choose to become a voice of hope, know that it is never easy but always worth it. You may be someone who thinks that you can't dream because of your wounds, but we are all wounded healers. Sometimes those of us who have been wounded bring the greatest healing to others.

God has given us all an opportunity to give ourselves away; it is our mission to see how we can do so. Only then will our jadedness begin to fall away. Then, once our focus is finally off ourselves and onto God and other people, we will at last be out of the cycle of cynicism and despair. We will have found a new way of living. And we will be equipped to point others to that same way of life.

Henri Nouwen's book *The Wounded Healer* is a great further resource about the concept of wounding.

God doesn't want a person to wait until they are over their wounds to begin to minister to others. According to Nouwen, pain is actually what equips a person to be a minister.

Breaking the Cycle

○ Maybe your experience with *Jaded* has led you to conclude that you need to talk to a counselor. It will take courage, but continue your recovery from past wounds by seeking out help.

○ Start to engage the person you think God wants you to believe in. Begin small—how about coffee this week?

"NO DOUBT ABOUT IT! GOD IS GOOD—

GOOD TO GOOD PEOPLE, GOOD TO THE GOOD-HEARTED.

BUT I NEARLY MISSED IT, MISSED SEEING HIS GOODNESS.

I WAS LOOKING THE OTHER WAY, LOOKING UP TO THE PEOPLE

AT THE TOP, ENVYING THE WICKED WHO HAVE IT MADE,

WHO HAVE NOTHING TO WORRY ABOUT, NOT A CARE IN THE WHOLE

WIDE WORLD . . .

WHEN I WAS BELEAGUERED AND BITTER, TOTALLY CONSUMED BY ENVY,

I WAS TOTALLY IGNORANT, A DUMB OX IN YOUR VERY PRESENCE.

I'M STILL IN YOUR PRESENCE, BUT YOU'VE TAKEN MY HAND.

YOU WISELY AND TENDERLY LEAD ME, AND THEN YOU BLESS ME.

YOU'RE ALL I WANT IN HEAVEN! YOU'RE ALL I WANT ON EARTH!

WHEN MY SKIN SAGS AND MY BONES GET BRITTLE,

GOD IS ROCK-FIRM AND FAITHFUL.

LOOK! THOSE WHO LEFT YOU ARE FALLING APART!

DESERTERS, THEY'LL NEVER BE HEARD FROM AGAIN.

BUT I'M IN THE VERY PRESENCE OF GOD—

OH, HOW REFRESHING IT IS!

I'VE MADE LORD GOD MY HOME.

GOD, I'M TELLING THE WORLD WHAT YOU DO!"

PSALM 73:1-3, 21-28, THE MESSAGE

NOTES

WHAT IS THREADS?

WE ARE A COMMUNITY OF YOUNG ADULTS—

people who are piecing the Christian life together, one
experience at a time. We're rooted in Romans 12 and
Colossians 3. We're serious about worshipping God with our
lives. We want to understand the grace Jesus extended to
us on the cross and act on it. We want community, need to
worship, and aren't willing to sit on our hands when the world
needs help. We want to grow. We crave Bible study that raises
questions, makes us think, and causes us to own our faith.
We're interested in friendships that are as strong as family
ties—the kind of relationships that transform individuals
into communities.

Our Bible studies are built for young adults, featuring flexible
formats with engaging supplemental video and audio, four- to
six-week sessions to fit into busy schedules, and supplemental
resources for members and leaders online. These discussion-
driven studies intentionally foster group and individual
connections and encourage practical application of Scripture.

We don't expect you to come up with the tools you need to lead these engaging
discussions in your communities on your own. We've designed a separate **Leader Kit**
—or expansion pack as we like to call it—that contains all the stuff you normally have
to go out looking for when you want to explore a topic. Purchase the Kit and you'll
receive theme-related videos, audio clips, and music in formats that are flexible for
your group, along with a **Leader Guide** in PDF format and other articles and tools
that encourage practical application of Scripture. You'll also find topical articles, staff
and author blogs, podcasts, and lots of other great resources at:

THREADSMEDIA.COM

STOP BY TO JOIN OUR ONLINE COMMUNITY
AND COME BY TO VISIT OFTEN!

GET UNCOMFORTABLE:
SERVE THE POOR. STOP INJUSTICE.
CHANGE THE WORLD ... IN JESUS' NAME.
BY TODD PHILLIPS

Phillips guides you to understand how your faith in Christ and concern for the poor go hand-in-hand. As he examines God's character and perspective regarding poverty and injustice, he offers an understanding of what God calls you to do, along with practical ways to impact culture by caring for "the least of these."

TODD PHILLIPS *is the teaching pastor of Frontline, the young adult ministry of McLean Bible Church near Washington D.C. His passions are teaching the people of God and sharing the Gospel with those who aren't yet Christians. He is the author of* Spiritual CPR: Reviving a Flat-lined Generation.

CONNECT THE DOTS:
DISCOVERING GOD'S ONGOING WILL IN YOUR LIFE
BY MIKE HURT

What if finding God's will in your life is about a lot more than just finding some answers to big questions? This six-session study will help develop people more committed to walking with Jesus than just knowing the next step in their life journey.

MIKE HURT *is the director of community campus development at McLean Bible Church just outside of Washington, D.C. As a leading thinker and trainer for small group ministry, Mike is passionate about helping people connect in authentic relationships with God and each other.*

THE EXCHANGE:
TIRED OF LIVING THE CHRISTIAN LIFE ON YOUR OWN?
BY JOEL ENGLE

An exploration of Romans 6, 7, and 8, this study will help you understand that the power of the Christian life is not found in yourself or religious activity, but in "exchanging" your life for the life of Jesus Christ. You'll learn how to overcome sin and personal hang-ups through a life of dependency on Christ.

JOEL ENGLE *is a worship communicator who uses his gifts to impact lives and glorify God. In* The Exchange, *Joel shares his own story of finally understanding what the Christian life is all about and learning to depend solely on Christ. Visit Joel online at* joelengle.com.

IN
TRANSIT

WHAT DO YOU DO
WITH YOUR WAIT?

MIKE HARDER

Table of Contents
INTRANSIT: WHAT DO YOU DO WITH YOUR WAIT?

0017

EXIT
TIME

(CAR)

Welcome to InTransit

A TRIP IN DISCOVERING HOW TO MAKE THE MOST OF YOUR WAIT

Whether grounded at the airport or standing in the never-ending line at the DMV, we're familiar with the waiting game.

We may not like it, but it's something we do. For most of our lives, we've been waiting for something — a driver's license, a graduation, a birthday, a spouse, a job … And from here until Eternity, we'll be waiting for whatever's next.

Author Mike Harder is a professional "waiter." He's logged countless hours at the airport on mission trips. He's stood in eternally long lines for that perfect cup of coffee. He's waited on God to bring the right job, right group of friends, and right girl. And he waited for God to give him new purpose after realizing that the plans he had for his life, while good, were not the plans God had in mind.

InTransit: What Do You Do with Your Wait? traces the lives of a few of the Bible's most influential men — Joseph, David, and Jesus — who were promised great things concerning their lives and waited, sometimes painfully, to see God's promises come to pass. What was true for them remains true for you today: There is great purpose in the waiting.

Like any great journey in life, you don't want to wait alone — and you don't want to go through this study alone. So grab some friends, wrangle a leader from your church, and figure out a consistent time to meet together to talk, process, and pray about what you're learning.

Here's a great tip: read the session you're going to talk about before you get together with your group; that way, you'll be better prepared to inject your ideas into the discussion. Others will be counting on hearing your insight, wisdom, and experiences as well as what you're hearing from God.

At the end of each session, you'll see a section called "In the Meantime …" The ideas listed there can help you connect with and process what you're reading. So, take advantage of those every chance you get before your group meeting. Finally, there are some really cool pages for journaling in the back of this book. We've provided those because we believe you're going to have a lot to think about and say to God — and yourself — throughout this study. So you don't forget any of the good (and, OK, possibly difficult) stuff, write it down, draw it out, whatever you need to do process what you're discovering about yourself and your wait. (Check out the article on the follow pages for ideas to get started on your journal.)

Thanks for joining us — it's going to be an exciting wait!

Life is more than food, and the body more than clothes. Consider the ravens: They do not sow or reap, they have no storeroom or barn; yet God feeds them. And how much more valuable

Word Release
FREEING YOURSELF UP TO JOURNAL
by Jennifer McCaman

Very simply, if you can tell the truth, you can journal. A lot of times journaling is seen as girly or something presidents do for posterity's sake. Actually, journaling can be a simple and powerful way to grow in your spiritual life. For me, it provides a way to channel my frustrations, hopes, and opinions — and it's just between God and me.

When I first started journaling, I was always formulaic. I made each entry the same, and I'd only write about the events of my day. It became a dreaded obligation. Gradually, I learned that journaling shouldn't be like homework. The only rule of journaling is honesty. You might wonder *who* would lie in a journal? More than the absence of lies, journaling requires honesty that dives beneath the surface to the heart of who you are and what God is doing in your life. Writing connects me with God because it keeps me focused. Sometimes if I start praying silently or read a long Scripture passage, I'll suddenly find myself thinking about ice cream or the movie I saw last night. Journaling can help sift through your prayers and Bible study. You're also more likely to retain information (like Scripture) when you engage multiple senses while studying.

Journaling is a great way to see where God has been active in your life. Sometimes in the middle of a trial, I forget that God has been faithful in many past struggles. The enemy loves to blind us to the past triumphs of God in our lives. It's great to open a journal and renew my confidence that God will take care of me this time too.

Bottom line — journaling allows you to take off your image before God. He loves you and longs to have an intimate relationship with you. When you write, you don't have to sugarcoat, downplay, or avoid any part of who you are. You have the freedom to be completely vulnerable — something that will bring you unbelievably close to God.

If you've never journaled before, great! You won't have to unlearn any bad habits. I challenge you to use this study to launch your personal times with God. Take 15 to 20 minutes daily to practice journaling your reactions, thoughts, and conversations with God. If you invest honestly, you will grow more than you ever imagined.

> "If I don't write to empty my mind, I go mad." — Lord Byron

JOURNALING IS BENEFICIAL BECAUSE IT:

- Allows you to track your spiritual growth
- Connects you to God
- Focuses your thoughts on God
- Helps you to reflect, release, and praise God
- Uncovers your unknown needs and desires
- Reduces stress (kind of like free therapy)
- Lets you explore specific ways you can put Scripture into action now

JOURNALING IS NOT:

- Keeping a diary
- A chronological account of your day (6 a.m. woke up, 6:45 a.m. fed dog, etc.)
- The memoirs you hope will be published after you die
- For anyone but you and God

JOURNALING TIPS:

- Find a specific time and place to think and write where you are undisturbed.

- Try to be consistent. If you miss a few days, don't beat yourself up.

- Buy an inexpensive or plain notebook. You'll be more likely to be honest without the fear of goofing up a brand new journal. (You already have journal pages right here in the back of this book.)

- Not a writer? Not a problem. Fill your journal with pasted pictures, artwork, or random drawings that inspire you or represent what you're feeling. Also mind-maps and cognitive webs can be a great way to organize your thoughts.

  (Check out *http://en.wikipedia.org/wiki/Mind_map* for "how to" instructions and examples of different maps.)

- Write by hand if possible. It's OK to type, but there's something powerful about a record in your own handwriting.

- Write stream-of-consciousness style. Don't worry about punctuation, spelling, or organization.

WHAT DO I WRITE ABOUT?

- Thoughts, feelings, experiences from the day
- Reactions to Scripture, or impressions you had when reading a certain passage
- Prayers, questions, praises to God
- Frustrations or fears
- Blessings: how God showed Himself to you in a specific way

"Fill your paper with the
breathings of your heart."
— William Wordsworth

IF YOU GET STUCK, THINK ABOUT THESE QUESTIONS:

- What experiences led you to where you are now?
- What questions would you really like to ask God?
- Are there any past choices that are holding you back?
- What event in your life brought you to Christ?
- What great joys (or deep lows) have you experienced in your life?
- What blessings are you most thankful for right now?

Happy journaling!

Jennifer McCaman is a freelance writer from Smyrna, Tennessee.
After graduating from Samford University, she is happily
journaling her way through her first year of marriage.
As the wife of a student minister, Jennifer fills her
life with music, pizza, and a few hundred teenagers.

In the Waiting Room

In the spring of 2005, having seen the effects of the tsunami that rocked Southeast Asia, our church commissioned me to lead a team that would provide aid to a very remote and affected area on the island of Sumatra. We had an incredible time of service (minus the modern comforts of air conditioning, hot water, and walls). But when it was time to go home, we hit a roadblock.

In most emerging countries, air transportation to rural areas is sketchy, at best. Due to the damage to the country's infrastructure, we were told that getting a flight back would be hit or miss.

Minutes soon turned into hours and frustrations started to mount in the 100-degree heat. Slowly melting into a puddle of sticky goo, I got an epiphany: *I really hate waiting!*

Now I have always been somewhat driven and impatient, but my loathing for *having to wait* grew to new dimensions. In the soup of delirious thoughts floating through my head, I wondered why waiting is such a terrible thing.

Have you ever been stuck somewhere that left you incredibly frustrated? The duration of your wait may have caused emotions to simmer to the surface. I personally feel like I have been waiting my entire life for stuff; silly stuff, like the doctor (even when I arrived on time), or the bathroom when my sister was taking forever , or for much more serious stuff like the right job, getting things right with a friend, or the right person to marry.

I believe that, regardless of where we are in life, we are all waiting for something — for whatever is next. This can be a major issue, a gaping hole in our lives, in our "happiness quest" that gnaws at us like a scavenging rodent chewing on some Limburger.

Some of you have been waiting a long time for your issue or situation to be resolved, others for a much shorter time, but all of you are asking the same questions: *What should I be doing differently? When is this going to end? Did I totally miss my chance? Why is this happening to me? Is there some kind of sin or shortcoming in my life that is keeping me from achieving happiness or the thing I desire most?*

In the Waiting Room

Be assured you are not alone; we are all waiting for what is next in our lives. The *what* may be different for you than it is for your roommate or best friend or coworker or the others in your group. Having other people to walk through the wait with you is extremely important.

As you go through this study, ask God to build and strengthen the relationships within your group. Ask Him also to open your heart and mind to the truth He wants to reveal to you during this experience. As these things register, jot down what you are thinking, feeling, and learning in the journal at the back of this book (it starts after Session 6). Refer to it often and ask God for wisdom on how to deal with the stuff He's revealing to you. And don't forget to share what He's telling you with others in your group. They will be a source of great encouragement to you. Remember: you are not alone!

Just to get started, try answering the questions in the space below.

> Write down three things you are waiting for right now.
> Next to each, note how long you've been waiting for them
> to be resolved:

Watch "Bus Stop" during your first study group session. Which character do you relate to most?

> Share two of these with your group as you are comfortable.
> If it's too personal, don't worry about sharing. Just record them
> in your journal.

TIME IS WASTING AWAY

Because waiting is extremely taxing, it's hard to avoid thinking about the issues for which we desire true resolution. We numb ourselves to our own realities by over scheduling our lives; then, we're so busy doing things, we don't have any time to dwell on what is frustrating us.

Maybe you end up watching a lot of television or just hang out by yourself at a coffee shop. As a result you avoid meeting new people. Or, you may go the opposite direction and try to solve things yourself, tackling every situation with total independence.

Every once in a while, however, a moment of silence sneaks in and we are faced with reality and all the emotional frustration and loneliness that a wait often brings — and then, the questions rush in.

I know that you try to escape and numb out of stuff in your life; I know because I do it, too. In fact, sometimes it can be fun to numb out — but it's not healthy. The first way to get past this is to come face-to-face with what you're doing and why.

> List two or three ways that you numb out. Go ahead — elaborate:

> Why do you think that you look for escape?

> Share one of your 'numb-out techniques' with the group.

def·i·ni·tion
/num/
to make incapable of action or of feeling emotion; lacking or deficient in emotion or feeling; indifferent

HERE'S THE TRUTH(S)

Bummed out yet? Don't worry, there is good news! First of all, you aren't the first to go through this situation, so you're in great company. There are many godly people, from biblical times to the here-and-now, who have had to wait a long time to see their hopes and dreams come true — so there is no shame in waiting.

Second, there is purpose behind your wait and there is a way to wait with hope. Believe it or not, there is a way to be a proactive waiter. In fact, three great truths about waiting were modeled in the lives of David, Joseph, and Jesus as they followed their life missions:

Truth 1: The waiting can't be about the wait.

Truth 2: You can't short-circuit the wait.

Truth 3: God builds into you during the wait.

Over the next three sessions, we'll process these truths together. But for now, we're going to meet some guys from the Bible who waited well. We'll be learning a lot about them and how God used them — and their waits — in really significant ways.

CHARACTER STUDY

Now depending on how knowledgeable you are about the Bible, you may be familiar with these guys, or you may not know them very well at all. So here's a brief rundown. If you want to learn more, check out the sidebars on the pages of this book to learn more about them and the time in which they lived.

David was a king in Israel about 1000 B.C. He is widely regarded as being the greatest king ever in the history of Israel. He's famous in current history because he is credited with writing many of the Psalms. He's also a popular guy with children because of his battle with the giant warrior Goliath.

But David had a huge wait in his life. He was promised the kingdom when he was a young man at the age of 13 and had to wait 17 years before he received the crown. There were lots of obstacles that he had to face, and through those he learned how to trust God.

Joseph lived about 500 years earlier than David, and had to face many overwhelming odds to find success in life. Yet he managed to keep his integrity and his relationship with God intact. He had several opportunities

def·i·ni·tion
/säm/

a well-known book in the Old Testament made up of 150 songs, poems, and prayers; the word "psalms" comes from a Greek word that referred to songs that were accompanied by stringed instruments.

to take advantage of situations that he probably could have gotten away with, but Joseph submitted to God's will and timing instead. He is also well-known for his coat of many colors and eventually served as counselor to the Pharaoh of Egypt.

The third person we'll examine is the most well-known and controversial person who has ever lived; in fact, more has probably been written about **Jesus** than anyone else. Although Jesus was fully God, as a human, He still faced a wait. He had an incredibly urgent mission — to save the world from sin and death — but waited until the right time to bring it about.

David and Joseph may seem larger than life, fortified with character and abilities you think you could never achieve, but as you study them, take comfort in knowing that they struggled as they waited on God (often for long periods of time) to see their hopes fulfilled. Jesus faced rejection and temptation — things you've undoubtedly faced yourself.

It's my sincere desire that this study provides hope for your future and a very doable plan of action in the now despite your periods of waiting. To make it through, however, you need to harness the power of faith. Now you probably think you understand faith pretty well, but often it's a little more difficult to really grasp than we like to admit.

My friend Andy says that the distance between a promise and its completion is faith. That makes sense to me, because I have seen huge distances between promises and their fulfillment in my own life. I have discovered that sometimes I just have to trust in the plan that God has for me — but that can be really difficult to actually do.

"Now faith is being sure of what we hope for and certain of what we do not see" (Hebrews 11:1-3).

> **What do you think about having to trust God with your desires and goals for the future?**

Through the next five sessions, I pray that you will gain confidence that you can trust this unseen God with your wait and that He is certain and true — not something that is elusive or untrustworthy.

What would your life look like if you waited differently than you have been?

Download the *InTransit* playlist. Get the list from your group leader or at *www.threadsmedia. com/media*. Make it your "soundtrack" for this study.

It's Not Terminal
The movie *The Terminal* exemplifies the agony of waiting. The story's protagonist (Tom Hanks) travels to America to fulfill a promise made to his father. While he is in the air, his country's government is overthrown, stranding him in an airport. Despite the sudden halt of his plans, Viktor determines to keep his promise. It's an inspiring, yet quirky film you just might all be able to identify with.

PANIC ROOM?

I remember as a kid having to wait for my mom in the car when she went into a store to grab an item quickly. Even as a 10-year-old, I had developed a healthy aversion to shopping, and it was more fun to mess around with the radio and listen to music that Mom didn't think was appropriate. Usually, at some point while I was rocking out to Madonna, Guns N' Roses, or the Beach Boys (I was real hard core in back in the day!), I would forget what Mom looked like that day — what was most distinguishable about her from a distance or the way she had dressed that day.

My imagination would play tricks on me as panic started to set in; weird questions would surface, like: *Maybe she left me? Maybe she forgot where she parked?* Just when I was about to crack, she would appear, cruising effortlessly through the crowded parking lot to save the day. Relief would settle in, and the world felt OK again.

In the same way, many of us panic when we have to wait for a long period of time for the things we expect to happen in life. We tend to forget what God looks like — not what we have been taught about Him in Sunday School — but rather, what it's like to relate to Him, to feel Him near. Panic then rises in our lives like a flood of despair.

What can help you *not* forget who God is and what He looks like? That's a really tough question. The following are a few things that I think might help. Be forewarned; these aren't quick fixes or magical solutions. You won't be able to figure all this out in one sitting.